THE DINOSAUR STRAIN

Mark Brown is founder and Managing Director of Innovation Centre Europe Ltd, an organisation researching and promoting best creativity and innovation practice in organisations. He is also an Associate Faculty member at Henley Management College, United Kingdom, and co-founder of the European Innovation Project at the College.

His life divides between consultancy and presentations around the world, writing management books and articles, and continuing research at King's College, London University and Henley about why some individuals and organisations are more creative and innovative than others.

His last major publication is *The Dinosaur Strain*, 1988, and forthcoming titles include *Your Creative Edge*, Kogan Page, 1994, and *Super Creative Teams*, Kogan Page, 1994. He has also produced two videos *Ideas Into Action*, Melrose, 1993 and *The Blue Movie: Generating Great Ideas*, Melrose, 1994.

By the same author:

Memory Matters
Left-Handed: Right-Handed

Forthcoming book titles:

Your Creative Edge, Kogan Page, 1994
Super Creative Teams, Kogan Page, 1994
Successful Innovation, Kogan Page, 1994

Software:

Brian
Jackpot

Training packages:

Quality and Ingenuity Initiative
So You Think You're a Good Judge of Character
Winning Teams
Ideas into Action Teams

Video:

Ideas into Action, Melrose, 1993
The Blue Movie: Generating Great Ideas, Melrose, 1994

THE DINOSAUR STRAIN

THE SURVIVOR'S GUIDE TO PERSONAL
AND BUSINESS SUCCESS

Mark Brown

INNOVATION CENTRE EUROPE LTD

© Innovation Centre Europe Ltd 1993

This edition first published in 1993 by
Innovation Centre Europe Ltd
Winton House
Alfriston
Polegate
East Sussex
BN26 5UH

Second impression 1994

Designed by Clarke Williams

All illustrations not specified in the
Acknowledgements list by Ray Smith

Cover design by Peter Till

Cover design by Max Fairbrother

Printed and bound in Great Britain

CONTENTS

To
Father, Karen, Allen and Pete

THANKS

There are numerous friends and colleagues who have helped develop and elaborate the ideas in this book. There are then even more people whose breadth and depth of knowledge and insight goes before me and every other writer. I, simply, therefore, thank all members of both groups.

I would, in addition, like to thank co-director, Ian Taylor, and Dr Christopher Dewberry. When I describe certain concrete examples of 'tickling dinosaurs', I am sometimes describing a collaborative effort. So 'I', on certain occasions, means Ian and myself, or Chris and myself. I am precluded from saying 'we' as this refers, in other contexts, to 'the reader and others' and would create confusion.

The He/She Problem

As yet, there seems no stylistic convention that elegantly avoids apparent or actual sexism in the English language. The words 'he', 'person' and 'individual', etc., are therefore used to designate men and women, equally.

As part of this book concerns itself with prejudice, I apologise in advance for any prejudices I unwittingly display. The section in Chapter 4, entitled 'Only Bigots Say They Have No Prejudices' may offer some interesting insights into your own prejudices. I continue to learn about my own.

ACKNOWLEDGEMENTS

Acknowledgement and thanks are gratefully made as follows:

1. For the 'Hidden Man', page 24, from Porter, P. B. *The American Journal of Psychology*, Vol. 67, 1954, p. 550 – thanks to and reprinted by permission of the University of Illinois Press.

2. For the 'Puzzle-Picture', page 26, from *The American Journal of Psychology*, Vol. 64, 1951, p. 432, after Dallenbach – thanks again to and reprinted by permission of the University of Illinois Press.

3. The 'Young Girls/Old Women', page 30, thanks to and reprinted by permission of the artist, George Downes.

4. For the 'Man Girl' figure, page 33, from *Perception and Psychophysics*, Vol. 4, No. 3, pp.189–192 – thanks to and reprinted by permission of Psychonomic Society, Inc. And thanks to the author of the article, Gerald Fisher.

5. For the 'Hidden Man Revealed', page 27, from Abercrombie, M. L. J. *The Anatomy of Judgement*, Hutchinson, 1960 – thanks to and reprinted by permission of Century Hutchinson Ltd.

6. For 'Darwin', page 49, thanks to and reprinted by permission of the artist, Siné.

Many thanks to Brian Rutherford for the images in the section 'Only Bigots Say They Have No Prejudices' pp. 71-80.

Certain short sections from the Introduction and Chapter 10 were first published in *International Management Development Review* 1986 and are reprinted with permission from Sterling Publications Limited.

Also thanks to *Management Today*, published by Management
Publications Limited, a subsidiary of Haymarket Publishing
Group Ltd., for permission to quote from material originally
published by them.

The videos, *Ideas Into Action* and *The Blue Movie: Generating
Great Ideas*, are available in the UK and worldwide from
Melrose - tel + 44 71 627 8404.
In the USA they are available from CRM - tel +1 619 431 9800.

FOREWORD

by Robert Heller

All managers fail. That is, neither they nor their organisations achieve either what managers want themselves, or what the outside world expects. Yet all managers succeed. That is, most of the time they achieve results that are broadly acceptable to them, and to an outside world whose most important inhabitants are the customers. Enormous effort is expended on trying to narrow the distance between success and failure: and most of that effort is wasted. The drive for total success is frustrated, not by the competition or the environment, but by the internal blockages of the organisation–which means those individuals who comprise it, not only as individuals, but as groups.

This analysis, far from being dispiriting, is full of hope. Knowledge of the human mind and its behaviour, which has improved immeasurably in modern times, means that the blockages can be cleared. This book rightly stresses the immense value of 'positive doubt' in breaking the pattern of frustration that creates the corporate dinosaur, unable to move from adequate success/partial failure into new and more productive modes. But there are few doubts or secrets about the sources of what Mark Brown calls 'Type 1' thinking, with its rigidity and arrogance – or its cure: how to convert its victims (the corporate majority) into 'Type 2' thinkers, with open and unstuck minds. Nor do frustrated managers have to wait for the organisation to move: they can move themselves by reading this book, answering its questionnaires and doing the fascinating exercises that will open their minds and their opportunities.

Not only is unsetting the mind productive and profitable, it is fun. And yet individuals, like their groups and organisations, may find the effort to change intimidating. Why? The strength of prejudices and predispositions, however idiotic, is enormous, because they run deep into the personality. The difficulty is similar to that which stops executives from approaching their companies as customers (which, of course, they are for other people's goods and services, and very possibly for their own). The lessons to be learnt from phone calls unanswered, orders mishandled and information unavailable are obvious – which is precisely the point. The self-image of the company could not survive the obvious evidence of its inability to serve the customer well: faced with the choice between good service and a damaged self-image, the manager opts out.

Yet anybody who shows managers a list of key defects will get honest admissions that all or most of them exist inside the company. Why isn't action taken to eliminate the defects? Again, the mind-blocks come into play. Mark Brown isn't content, however, merely to show how the blockages form and can be overcome. He is intent on converting self-knowledge into corporate action, on overturning the inertia that is the dinosaur's main characteristic. Recognising what the customer wants, which the book rightly stresses throughout as the key to commercial success, is only the start: turning that key sets in motion a chain of action and reaction that challenges the corporate norms.

The challenge is inevitable, and so is failure to meet the challenge – if the potential challenger believes that the dinosaur characteristics are immutable. The chapter on 'Halos and Horns' makes remarkable, astounding and deeply instructive reading. People and organisations come to fit their labels: change the labels, turn the horns into halos, give the dog a good instead of a bad name, and you change the behaviour and the performance. The chairman who complains that his company can't find good managers is describing a bad company. Good ones create good managers by the way they are managed: not, as Mark Brown emphasises, by the way they are 'trained'. True, 'learning' is vital to management development; but that, if it doesn't mean management performance, means nothing.

Where the 'Dinosaur Strain' can be most damaging is in the arena of innovation. Plainly, an organisation whose individual and collective mind-sets act against meeting the existing objectives isn't likely to succeed at forming, let alone reaching, new ones. The highly practical section on using the new knowledge about thinking to achieve new, implemented ideas lays rightful stress on goals. Innovation isn't commonly thought of in terms of goal-setting: that idea alone, however, changes the perspective and improves the chances of success – especially if you follow Mark Brown's advice and work on one specific goal at a time. Too many statements of 'corporate mission' embody multiple objectives which muddy thought and increase the difficulty of obtaining the action that turns the half-failed dinosaur into the wholly successful modern animal.

But is whole success ever possible? The report quoted here on the failure rate of market forecasts – half of which prove wrong – is echoed in the shortfall of new products, corporate acquisitions and, very likely, all business enterprises, internal and external. The odds on human success seem to be 50–50 at best; but they are no more immutable than the organisation's resistance to change. The test involving counting the letter 'F', given on page 54, demonstrates the simple solution to this apparently complex issue. Most people fail the test: but there is a method which guarantees 100% success. You won't find it, however, without first stopping to think – try to rush the problem, and failure is almost guaranteed.

In business, 100% success is never possible: it cannot even be defined. But the total achievement of ambitious goals can certainly be achieved, and with a much greater frequency than half the time, by individuals and organisations who are prepared to work at it. 'Prepared' is the master word. This excellent book will prepare its readers, or rather users, to achieve optimum success for themselves and their organisations. The only catch is that you do have to 'work at it' – not by long and laborious hours, which are easy, but by concentrated and continuous effort to rid the marvellous human mind of its self-created impediments. That is by no means easy: but the pay-off, even from half-success, is wholly remarkable.

INTRODUCTION

The dinosaur strain is unmistakable. You can feel it within minutes of walking into the offices of any fossilising or stuck organisation. It makes you feel tired and weighed down. There is a lack of vitality, innovation, enjoyment and energy. It's not unlike depression.

Although dinosaurs were, in fact, a remarkably successful species, we tend to accept in common usage that 'to be a dinosaur' means to be a 'stick in the mud' and resistant to new ideas and change. That resistance is what you detect so quickly on encountering this type of dinosaur, whether in the form of an individual or company (or department or function). For some the dinosaur strain is in its early stages, with others you hear the creaking of rigor mortis.

You can detect the dinosaur strain in the person's eyes – tombstones! He or she is 'psychologically retired'. The body still moves, slowly at least, and the nose may twitch if a rise is mentioned. But that's about it.

You can equally easily detect the dinosaur strain within the organisation. Simply try suggesting a not too radical and new idea and watch the hundred instant ways the bureaucracy 'yes . . . buts' the suggestion. 'Interesting, write me a report on it . . . it's not your job to think about that . . . it would never work here . . . the unions/top management would never accept it,' etc. The organisation, its culture and people operate as an idea assassination mechanism.

There are then a whole range of other dinosaur indicators. For example, there is the general attitude towards customers. At best, they are inconvenient 'punters' who get in the way of the real work.

Inside the organisation, employees have 'I just work here' written all over them.

Different parts of the organisation compete with each other as though they were desperate rivals.

Excessive controls and bureaucracy leave managers feeling as if they were professional subordinates, left to manage by numbers. There are few *Homo sapiens*, mainly *Homo mechanici.*

Then there is an acute case of 'rigid fingers', where everybody points the finger of blame at someone else, all saying 'I'd love to but my boss . . .' or 'taking the effort is more trouble than it's worth' or 'don't rock the boat' or 'I've only got five/ten/twenty years to go'! All these fingers are finally pointing at top management and the Board, who in their turn bemoan the fact that there doesn't seem to be much innovation and energy around!

And most of all in the dinosaur organisation there simply is no *fun*! At least no productive fun, that is – some may get their kicks out of putting proverbial spanners in the works.

And sure enough, without fun, energy and innovation any organisation will begin to lose any leading or competitive edge it may have had. The dinosaur strain has set in.

But there are organisations, small, medium and enormous, which are alive, great fun to work within, and innovative as well. This book is about what you can do to ensure that you never become psychologically retired and that your organisation never becomes a dinosaur. That is unless it is already too late!

The 'How Never to Become a Dinosaur' solutions and ideas presented throughout this book are, however, neither simplistic nor very simple. Managers, quite rightly, have grown suspicious of instant pat formulae for corporate and personal success. The American business magazine *Business Week*[1] ran one issue with the cover '*Oops!*'. The cover and story considered what had happened to those successful companies which had 'starred' as example practitioners of the 'eight attributes of excellence' in the best-selling book *In Search of Excellence* by Peters and Waterman:[2]

According to studies by *Business Week*, management consultants McKinsey & Co., and Standard & Poor's Compustat Services Inc., at least 14 of the 43 'excellent' companies highlighted by Peters and co-author

Robert H. Waterman Jr. in their book just two years
ago have lost their lustre.[3]

The same article goes on to point out that perhaps the most
revered of management gurus, Peter Drucker, dismissed *In
Search of Excellence* as 'a book for juveniles'. Since that book
there has been a plethora of 'sons of' – Rocky 16, 17 and the
like. Many, likewise, have become best-sellers.

All these 'The Never Previously Disclosed Secrets of
Corporate Success and Longevity' books present a problem.
Whereas sound but heavyweight academic tomes rarely get
read by managers, these more popular ones do. And within
them there is probably very sound advice – yet, also, some
which is less than sound. The difficulty is the same as with
the Professor of Medicine who starts every new lecture
course by telling his students that half of what he will say will
be proved wrong – the other half right. The only problem is
that he doesn't know which is which. In business, it may
be that by the time we have found which half is right it will
be outdated and therefore useless.

Now, you may ask, why can't you make more of a
science of management – so that you can begin to predict
with a fair degree of certainty what will and won't succeed
in organisations? Well, first of all, every business is different.
An approach may work here but not there. Even the most
seemingly obvious of solutions, like penicillin, may help
some, but harm others.

Secondly, the world has a mischievous and recurrent
knack of changing! Disraeli said, 'Change is a constant.'
Perhaps today, with revolutionary and not simply evolutionary change, you need a new word to describe how
'change' itself is changing. The problem of thinking about
'change' as meaning only evolutionary change is that you
may feel that historical pattern and precedent is useful in
making sense of today and tomorrow. Undoubtedly this
can be so. For example, you may be able to understand the
past, to appreciate the present and so attempt to predict the
future. But the danger with all historical patterns is that they
can and do mislead, especially when you are faced with
revolutionary change. More than ever before, you need to
be suspicious of the usefulness of unexamined precedent.

And when it comes to quantum leaps, it may be that no precedent is appropriate.

So, for small-level change, incremental change, the word 'change' is appropriate, but for quantum change, be it social, moral, economic, industrial, political, even 'Megatrends'[4] will not do – that again may suggest understandable and predictable evolving patterns. You need to introduce a new word, more suggestive of revolutionary than of simple evolutionary or incremental change. In science there is the expression 'paradigm shift',[5] to describe the case where whole previous ways of seeing, thinking and behaving are now seen to be inappropriate. Paradigm shifts both in the world and in business are becoming the norm.

So as to capture the idea that *uncertainty is natural*, you need to 'reframe', that is redefine, the word 'doubt'. 'Doubt' is, perhaps, more often than not, associated in people's minds, with weakness and not strength. Here, we are not talking about neurotic self-doubt but of *positive doubt* that recognises the foolishness of arrogance and certainty in a world of never-ending flux.

In a world of paradigm shifts, those who win are those who thrive on positive doubt.[6] You cannot be certain of what to do next. You decide what to do on the basis of intelligent sensing (what is sometimes called 'right brain' thinking) and analysis (sometimes called 'left brain' thinking),[7] of what is happening now. You then act – and, in turn, lead and enthuse those around you. You may even enthuse and lead so convincingly that those around you believe you to be certain. But you know that any old fool can be certain – it takes courage both to doubt and act. Thus this book is in praise of *positive doubt*.

More and more often you find that when you ask any good consultant, management guru or academic a 'How to' question, you get a 'Well, *it all depends* . . .' answer. Contingency theory rules supreme.[8] The science of management, whose central quest is the producing of *general* rules, is at best, a difficult science, if a science at all, because organisations are unique and our times are without precedent.

The third reason why you can't make more of a science of management is because there are always several interacting factors in any organisation at any one time. For all practical purposes, therefore, it is impossible to carry out a controlled experiment, so as to establish what works and what doesn't. In a controlled experiment ideally you introduce or change one variable at a time, while keeping other variables constant – and so see what happens. In one business, for example, you might decide to introduce a completely new structure in the hope of improving organisational effectiveness. Such a change programme may coincide with an array of uncontrollable variables – the market place becomes more buoyant, a competitor launches an unexpected, new and challenging product, new legislation is rumoured, trade figures are better than expected, there is an inexplicable dip in exchange rates and, to cap it all, your marketing director leaves to join your prime competitor. A relationship, whether strong, weak or non-existent, between your restructuring of the organisation and any subsequent change in effectiveness, does not of itself imply or deny causation. And even if you do find a link between your changes and organisational effectiveness, this may be due to the Hawthorne effect,[9] which describes the way that *any change* can, for at least some time, have some positive effect.

This analysis may seem to suggest that there is no point in doing anything. Not so. My plea is for sound thinking before any action is taken so as to discover what action to take in the first place. You cannot prescribe in advance exactly what to do – because you do not know the nature of future events and environments.

You can, however, begin to consider at least one factor we know about – *people*. And it is people who create and change organisations. Therefore we want to understand what makes them tick, what helps them perform well and act in pursuit of new ideals and goals. *We may not know what the future holds, but we do know that human beings will be central players*. Therefore this book considers some knowledge we have about ourselves. Such knowledge and understanding can help generate the appropriate solutions given whatever future. Although perhaps overquoted, the best advice surely is to teach a hungry man to fish for himself, rather than give him just the one fish. (In all honesty, anyway, I couldn't be

sure I was offering a 'sound' fish – it might so easily turn out
to be a red herring!) *The Dinosaur Strain* therefore considers
some of the skills of fishing.

References

1. 'Who's Excellent Now?' *Business Week*, November 5, 1984, pp.
   76–78.
2. Peters, T. J. & Waterman Jr., R. H. *In Search of Excellence*, Harvard
   University Press, 1981.
3. 'Who's Excellent Now?'. Ibid.
4. Naisbitt, J. *Megatrends*, Macdonald and Co., 1984. A fascinating
   guide to ten global trends affecting work and private life.
5. Kuhn, T. S. *The Structure of Scientific Revolutions*, University of
   Chicago Press, 1962, 1970. The seminal work on deep mind-sets
   in science – that are so deep that normally we don't, and often
   can't, even see them. Not a simple read but extremely rewarding.
6. Peters, T. *Thriving on Chaos*, Macmillan, London, 1988. It will
   be instructive to see how this book's prescriptions are reviewed
   in some five years. A good clear read with some very practical
   advice.
7. Ornstein, R. H. *The Psychology of Consciousness*, W. H. Freeman,
   1972. This book excited much public interest in the left and right
   brain research.
   Brown, M. *Left Handed: Right Handed*, David and Charles, 1979.
   Here I tried to provide an overview of the research on the
   reasons for left- and right-handedness, the functions of the left
   and right sides of the brain, and how the integration of 'leftism'
   and 'rightism' might help cure some educational and social ills.
   A general point of warning about the popular understanding of
   the ideas of 'left' and 'right' brain thinking is that it is much
   more complicated than often represented to be. The model is,
   however, symbolically interesting.
8. For example, see, Tosi, Jr., H. L. & Slocum, Jr., J. W.'Contingency
   Theory: Some Suggested Directions', *Journal of Management*, 1984,
   10, No. 1.
9. The original research into the Hawthorne effect can be found in
   Roethlisberger, F. J. & Dickson, W. J. *Management and the Worker*,
   Harvard University Press, Cambridge, Mass., 1939.

CHAPTER ONE

Dissecting the Dinosaur

AS YOU READ THIS CHAPTER you may want to consider the extent to which the descriptions of the 'Dinosaur Strain' apply to you and your organisation. You can record your subjective score after each description. However don't kid yourself. This book is not for the faint-hearted. Watch out if you consistently score yourself more favourably than you score your organisation!

Yes . . . But

'Yes . . . but', he said, again and again, interminably. There was no way I could encourage the technical director of that very large paint manufacturer to think afresh, to entertain a new idea. By the look of him he might well have had hardened arteries. There seemed little doubt he had hardened mental categories. If you suggested an idea that didn't fit his very stuck mental grid he simply pipped it out. The only ideas he seemed able to accept were those that already fitted his 'grid of experience'. Then, of course, he said 'We've already had that idea. I thought you were meant to help us be more innovative'! He was exquisitely stuck in his own world, believing his world to be *the* world. And he seemed quite comfortable scurrying about in his fur-lined conceptual ruts. As long as he was responsible for technical innovation, I reflected, his company would continue to lose market share to more innovative competitors.

Some readers may think that there is much to be said for the scalpel-sharp analytical 'yes . . . but' which can help improve the quality of otherwise fuzzy thinking. This is sometimes true. That is, the constructive 'yes . . . butter' can be a wonderful sounding-board. Sadly, however, many 'yes . . . buts' simply reflect an outlook hidebound by precedent and the difficulty many of us have in entertaining the new. The 'yes . . . but' is destructive as it stops the exploration of the new. Our 'grids of experience' usually only allow space for those ideas that slip between the bars of our mental prisons.

To entertain the new means that you are vulnerable. You have to be able to tolerate uncertainty and ambiguity, and to entertain positive doubt, while the new idea is conceived and gestated. The new idea requires the nurturing of open and imaginative minds and not the cold, harsh hammer of the all-knowing, closed, arrogant and destructive 'yes . . . but'.

So how would you rate your own organisation? And what about yourself?

(1)   **Organisation**

Those around you 'Yes . . .   Those around you
but' ideas to death   encourage new ideas

0   5   10

(A)   **Yourself**

I tend to kill   I encourage myself and others
off ideas   to come up with new ideas

0   5   10

Goddam Punters

Try driving to Terminal 4, at Heathrow Airport, London. Inside the terminal 4 complex you reach a roundabout. The sign that indicates the way to the terminal itself is absurdly small. Furthermore it is obscured by a post right in your line of vision. So all except the most perspicacious might circle round twice or more.

Finally you turn off into the main complex only to find yourself confronted with a choice of four lanes. The overhead signs have so much writing you want an instant speed-reading course! You have seconds to decide. You are craning your neck to read this mass of information. Simultaneously you are meant to avoid the dithering car in front of you!

There is a large body of research readily available on how long it takes to read signs at various speeds and how to make information as accessible as possible. There may be good reasons for the layout being as it is, but it seems to me that those responsible for this, and much other, signing are too close to the problem to be able to appreciate it from the point of view of the first-time user. They have become stuck in their own worlds and so may have begun to believe that their world is *the* world. So much signing, from airports through to the roads generally, reveals a lack of clarity and impact, that, at times you wonder if the original intention was to mislead!

Individuals who are stuck in seeing things only from their own point of view are called egocentric and companies who are the same are called 'company-centric'. Successful companies are the opposite, that is, they are customer-centric.

Heathrow has for some time boasted the idea of being *the* international airport of the world. I recall sitting in one of the airport's restaurants and watching a Japanese businessman trying to order some breakfast. He asked an Indian waitress to explain 'scrambled eggs'. She had little success in enlightening him. As I watched their faltering conversation I observed the menu card. The menu was written in English on just one side. The other side was blank and provided ample space for reproducing, at least in small print, the same menu in several other languages. The design said little for an international perspective!

This lack of customer and user awareness is infuriatingly common. There are numerous videos and video instruction booklets that over-tax your intelligence, unfriendly computers with hostile manuals, various telephone enquiry systems that rarely reply – and if answered often leave you on everlasting hold. Until the belated introduction of push-button telephones, the old dial-type phone would slide around the desk as you dialled, as though trying to escape you.

Successful organisations provide what the user, customer or consumer (or patient – oh yes, be forever patient) wants, when and how they want it. State-funded organisations that don't do this become unpopular, a joke or both; commercial set-ups that don't do this go broke. And sad it is that it takes quite so long for many of them to go under.

Apathy is often part of the problem. Many commercial organisations suffer from the 'failure of success'. This simply means that due to past success they carry on doing things in much the same old way. Public and professional bodies may suffer from the 'failure of monopoly' and have become seemingly sacrosanct and unchallengeable 'institutions'. Both have enough accumulated wealth, power or continuing state subsidy to perpetuate, for a time, their market life. Such dinosaurs often seem impervious to customer dissatisfaction. Moreover most dissatisfied customers still do not complain. Why bang your head against a brick wall!

Consumerism, however, is at long last beginning to have an impact on the old attitude of not complaining about shoddy goods and appalling service. The other day it took me thirty-seven minutes to get through to one particular department in one of London's biggest bookshops. I made a second call to the Chairman and suddenly there were profuse apologies and promises of no recurrence. A few weeks earlier, following the offhand behaviour of an aggressive salesman for a well-known French car manufacturer, I called the UK head office and asked to speak to the personnel director. The managing director of the outlet in question called me the next day.

The customer who complains is a real resource for any organisation. And yet the complaining 'punter' (which tells you all you need to know about how uncustomer-centric some organisations really are) is often perceived as a pain in the neck. The attitude expressed by the managing director of that car outlet was – 'We are successful enough so what is all the fuss about?' This was a clear example of the failure of success. I wonder how much longer his success will last.

If your company, and especially the marketing function, listened to all customer complaints and then acted on those relevant ones it would already be miles ahead of most of the competition.

If you want to be the leader of the pack, the competition that is, you have to go that one step further. You have to get into the customer's head and find out what it is they want and when and how they want it. You don't simply rely on putting things right once they've already gone wrong.

(2)   **The Customer's World**

We are geared to providing   We provide what the
what we want to provide   customer wants

0   5   10

(B)

I'm inclined to see things   I'm good at seeing
from my point of view   things from others'
                                    points of view

0   5   10

Drowning in Problems

Being customer-centric leads you straight into the next dimension by which you can judge if you are a dinosaur or not. Many organisations rely on the old saying that 'Necessity is the mother of invention'. That is, once there is a problem they might begin to think about things a bit – they might even manage to come up with a new idea (gagging the 'yes . . . butters' in the meantime). Now the problem with this firefighting attitude is that by the time there are problems you are usually losing market share. Other more progressive organisations have taken your position. So not only do you have to come up with the new winning idea but you then have to fight those who have moved in because of your complacency. This problem-solving orientation is typical of many an aspiring dinosaur.

The healthier animal, more dynamic and innovative, lives by a variation of 'Necessity is the mother of invention'. And it is a vital variation, which simply states:

'We can *never allow* necessity to be the mother of invention – we must invent/innovate *now!*'

Such an organisation is 'opportunity'-focused and not simply orientated towards problem-solving. The primary question at all times is 'What can you do that's new that the customer wants?' and/or 'What can you do differently that the customer wants?' There are then related questions to do with saving costs and increasing productivity. All such initiatives will help make you more price-attractive.

You work out what are the new ideas that will benefit your existing customers or attract new customers or both. You then evaluate those ideas (useful 'yes . . . butting' time). Finally but quickly you action those evaluated ideas. Then again and again. There is more of how to do this in Chapters 8 and 9.

It's so simple to say – opportunities and not just problems. Most people, however, are very biased towards problem-solving in the way they live their lives. Most only start to think in an imaginative way if there is a problem that presents itself. Rarely do you try to discover or invent a relevant problem – that is, seek out an opportunity.

(3)   **The organisation tends to be**

Problem-solving-focused   Opportunity-focused

0   5   10

(C)   **I am**

Problem-solving-focused   Opportunity-focused

0   5   10

There are then several aspects of the dinosaur strain that cluster under the general attitude of:

'I Just Work Here.'

I recall being asked to present a 'motivational' speech to the employees of a very large national petrol retailer. The company was pushing a new image, part of which was concerned with high-quality customer care along with having employees feel more involved in the company. I was therefore interested when a few days after my presentation I pulled into the forecourt of one of the company's petrol stations.

I filled up the car and started to check my water and tyre pressures. There was a water tap but no hose or container. The tyre pressure gauge gave readings for my tyres that suggested they should have already exploded. As I paid for the petrol I asked the cashier-cum-attendant about the lack of facilities. Having been reassured that he had tried to solve the first problem by supplying buckets which were always stolen, followed by milk bottles which also disappeared or got broken, he went on to say that the pressure gauge was a constant headache. He was a quiet, gentle man who seemed almost surprised that I was commenting on the lack of working facilities. As I turned to leave he looked up and said, as though to provide a total explanation, 'I just work here.' So much for customer care and a sense of personal involvement in running 'his' company. In no way did he think of it as 'his' company.

Now you can't really blame *him*. He may have felt uninterested in his job and company or powerless to do anything to bring about improvements or change.

Tombstones in the Eyes

One straightforward reason why you run into this 'I just work here' temperament (and, of course, there are lots of other ways of saying the same sort of thing – 'I've only got five/ten/twenty(!) years to go', 'taking the initiative is more trouble than it's worth', 'nobody listens', 'keep your head down') is round pegs in square holes. The individuals are simply not motivated. They are psychologically retired.

I remember visiting, as a consultant, the head office of a large finance company and waiting for one of four lifts to arrive. There were three young female employees (you could tell employees from visitors by the different badges worn) standing listlessly in front of one of the other lift doors. My lift arrived first and I pressed the 'hold' button and asked them if they wanted to come. They replied, again listlessly, that they would wait for the next lift. Now, granted, this may be a simple comment on me, but it's not as though they were even talking and enjoying themselves. Quite simply the act of waiting for a lift was apparently better fun than getting on with their work!

Simple you might say, 'motivate' them. Well, in reply to that suggestion, here is a glimpse of what should be blindingly obvious. *You cannot motivate people*, any more than you can 'learn' them. People are motivated in their own unique ways. People, under natural circumstances *want to do things*. They are all 'intrinsically' motivated. And if employees are not motivated to do their jobs it is simply because what makes them tick is not what they are asked to do in those jobs. Such people under-perform, often become stressed, are mentally or psychologically retired (day-dreaming is the preferred pastime) and often wonder what the hell they are doing wasting their lives doing such jobs.

Successful organisations employ all their people on the basis of matching the individual's intrinsic motivation to the right job. People then perform well and enjoy themselves – win, win.

(4)

| Many of our people are mentally retired | Our people are very well-matched to their jobs |

| 0 | 5 | 10 |

(D)

| I am mentally retired | I love my job |

| 0 | 5 | 10 |

'Hate the Place'

Individuals may love their jobs but hate the place – that is the organisation for which they work. Their own values and those of the organisation are at odds. A Christian manager who works for an armaments company may love his job because of the challenge, and yet find a mismatch between his creed and the organisation's business goal and values. Providing hardware for a possible Armageddon may sit uncomfortably with the tenet of 'Love thy neighbour'.

This issue of organisational values can seem rather elusive at first. You can accept the idea of people having different sets of values, or principles that guide behaviour. A fly-by-night second-hand car salesman may have very different values from a schoolteacher. But likewise organisations do have values, often implicit, and these vary from one outfit to another.

What might some of the Mafia's values be, for example? Perhaps 'loyalty', 'discretion' and 'material gain'. A Quaker company might have such values as 'care for its people' along with a sense of 'local and social responsibility'. Some companies make their values explicit. One such example is Apple Computer, whose stated values are: empathy for customers, achievement/aggressiveness, innovation/vision, quality/excellence, positive social contribution, individual performance, individual growth/reward, team spirit and lastly good management.

In many organisations, you may have to work there for some time before you find out what their real values are. And 'real values' is the important point. Many companies like to think, at least at board and senior management level, that they have clear values. Some of these may, however, only receive lip-service support. They are not manifest in the everyday activity of business life.

Tour operators/holiday companies may quickly compromise on a supposed value like 'the customer comes first' if it involves them flying near-empty planes out to various resorts. Rather than get the client straight to a resort, the same plane may touch down at several different airports in the UK to pick up more passengers before finally flying on to its intended destination. Fewer planes are used, so costs are cut, but first-pick-up passengers are hugely delayed in their final arrival because of this impromptu tour of the UK.

The value of 'social responsibility' is often compromised in many organisations as they realise that what is really meant is 'profit-related social responsibility'. Rarely will a company sponsor, say, the building of an art gallery, unless they can see hard cash benefits accruing.

So, although people may be motivationally matched to their individual jobs, their own values and those of the organisation may clash or diverge. Such individuals become apathetic about the organisation or they become agents for change by way of challenging the existing values. Which way they jump is discussed later. So the attitude of 'I just work here' may be a result of motivational mismatch or values mismatch or both.

(5) **The match between individuals' values and those of the organisation is**

Poor   Good

0   5   10

(E) **The match between my values and those of the organisation is**

Poor   Good

0   5   10

There is a third possible reason for this dissociation from the organisation.

Rigid Fingers

Yes, 'rigid fingers', that are always pointing the finger of blame at someone else, blaming that person or department or policy for why things cannot be done. And sure enough, the people doing the pointing will have the level below pointing up at them!

Rigid fingers mean that people feel 'disempowered'. They see themselves as pawns in someone else's chess game. Seeing themselves as powerless, they don't act and so confirm their sense of helplessness.

There are probably several interacting factors that give rise to this problem of rigid fingers. One reason is certainly to do with the organisation and its culture and another to do with the particular psychology of the individual.

The organisational problem is to do with structure and levels of authority and decision-making. Many organisations are still surprisingly pyramid-shaped, with tier after tier of minor through to major bureaucrat, often accompanied by different restaurants for different bands of the hierarchy. Those higher up in the organisation seem to feel that the higher the hierarchy the better!

Hand in hand with such a structure you usually find that decisions have to be referred up and up, even if in many cases the decision is trivial and any possible adverse outcome is inconsequential. Many managers are no more than professional subordinates. If it's round, put it in this tray, if it's square, put it in that tray, and if it's any other shape refer it up. In this way people are encouraged not to think and, God forbid, certainly not to act. Stick to your narrowly prescribed job description and don't venture out of that tight zone of very limited control. Certainly don't try and influence things. Under no circumstances show any initiative!

Then there is a psychological reason for rigid fingers. As examined later, in Chapter 10, some people, because of various early life experiences, develop a very disempowered sense of what is possible. Someone who is personally very disempowered lives in a world full of flashing neon 'No's'. They believe that what really make things happen are factors outside their control. Such people will often be strong believers in 'fate', 'luck' and 'chance'.

Either or both of these reasons can create rigid fingers so that the organisation lacks energy and initiative. What you tend to forget, however, is that whenever you point the finger of blame there are always three fingers pointing straight back at yourself. Only you can make the difference.

One clear indication of disempowered people is the way those people talk about their organisation. Often you find that people talk about their companies as though *they actually exist*, in the sense of having a life-form of their own. People talk about 'the company', 'the business', 'the partnership', 'the bank' as though they were some monolithic giant striding around the mid-Atlantic. A company is a mere legal notion. All that exists that matters is people. That's us! You are the organisation. However, trying to change this deeply entrenched fixed viewpoint or 'mind-set' can be really hard work.

(6)

Rigid fingers abound	Individuals show high
People feel disempowered	levels of initiative

0	5	10

(F)

I feel disempowered	I take a lot of
	initiatives

0	5	10

Mind-Sets Galore

'Mind-set' simply means a fixed and predominant way of thinking and seeing. Any mind-set reinforces itself as you 'construe' or make sense of your world in ways which support those underpinning deep assumptions or beliefs.

Many of the above dinosaur characteristics are themselves mind-sets – for example company-centricity. However, mind-set warrants a place in its own right.

After you have worked in an organisation or job for some time you become saturated by the standard ways of thinking. You become 'company blind'. Everything makes sense and seems appropriate. You begin to lose the positive irritant of the grit in the oyster, your imagination, vision and push for constructive change. 'Yes . . . but' often indicates deep mind-sets at work.

At a strategic level, top thinkers may have become stuck with their historical business definition. Charles Revson of Revlon cosmetics fame challenged the standard business definition of 'manufacturer of cosmetics' when he said: 'In the factory we produce make-up. In the store we sell hope.' This alternative way of thinking or 'reframing' clearly allows for more than simply the production of lipsticks.

Much market, financial and social trend information is of a 'soft' nature. That is, if you want to be a market leader, you have to be able to read what's going to happen some considerable time before it does. This enables you to respond proactively and not reactively to change. To detect such change you have to use your mental peripheral vision to detect those soft clues that are suggestive of emergent trends. Otherwise you start to miss out on new opportunities. The mind that is set, however, is blind to such soft information and only sees opportunities once they have passed. As one leading authority on creativity and innovation, Vincent Nolan, points out:

> And so it was with Chester Carlson, for example, who discovered and named the Xerographic copying process and spent twenty years hawking it round the major photographic and office equipment companies, all of whom turned it down. Until finally it

was taken up by a tiny photographic company who had the vision, but hardly the resources, to develop it into today's Xerox Corporation.[1]

In many ways, therefore, the most unstuck people in the world are children. They have that infuriatingly relevant knack of always asking 'Why do you do it that way?' Our mind-sets are instantly revealed in our reply 'Well, we've always done it that way.'

Mind-set is also the arch-enemy of creativity and innovation. Innovation is applied creativity. Many of us have a mind-set that limits 'innovation' to such functions as research and development and marketing. Innovation rightly includes *product* and *service* and *procedural* innovation and improvement. You can apply your creativity to coming up with new products *and* also to the question of 'How can you better present, package and deliver this product/service?' And of course you apply the same question about your internal customers. Yes, you have customers inside the organisation. If you are the finance department, for example, your customers are both inside and outside the organisation.

Lastly 'mind-sets' equip you very badly to deal with change. In the same way that many an army is brilliantly trained to fight the last and not the next war, so many companies are stuck with yesterday's patterns of thought. They see the world, their market and their customers through a grid that worked some ten years earlier. Today's unprecedented rate of change calls for minds that never become set. The intelligent unset mind is what business must have and yet rigid mind-sets are more often the norm in many organisations.

(7)

| People's minds are fairly set | People are very good at 'thinking afresh' |

| 0 | 5 | 10 |

(G)

My mind is fairly   I am very good at
set   'thinking afresh'

0   5   10

So here you have some seven deadly or rather dinosaur-
inducing sins. How have your scored your own organisation
and how about yourself? You can record the two totals
below:

My organisation:_____   Myself:_____

Many people find that their own score is significantly greater
than that for their organisation. What does this imply? Well
clearly you could be kidding yourself. People don't like to
think of themselves as dinosaurs, even though they may be.
Or, on the other hand, you may see yourself as an agent of
change inside a fairly stuck organisation.

   If you don't want to be or become a dinosaur, what
animal represents what *you* want to be? A leopard, a tiger,
a horse, an elephant? And is your organisation a dinosaur?
What animal represents the *organisation* that you most want
to work within? And if you are moderately happy with your
present organisation what can you do to shift yourself, your
colleagues and organisation in the direction of your most
desired animal?

References

1. Nolan, V. 'Open to Change.', MCB Publications, *Management
    Decision*, 1981, Volume 19, No. 2, p.14. This specific journal should
    have been a book. It would have been excellent. Vincent Nolan
    has long been the British leading light in the 'Synectics Inc.' use
    of 'analogies' for creative problem solving.

CHAPTER TWO

Type 1 and Type 2 Thinkers

Some people believe their world is *the* world. This is a fundamental mind-set – that is, a fixed and predominant way of thinking, and reveals itself in a range of expressions and opinions:

–   When it comes to new ideas, it's – 'There's nothing new under the sun.'
–   When it comes to disagreement, it may range from – 'You're right from your point of view, but your point of view is wrong,' to less politely, 'You must be mad, bad or evil.'
–   When it comes to the idea of personal change and development, it's 'I am as I am and no amount of thinking will change it.'

You quickly sense the extremity and stuckness of such a position, which from now on I will 'label' Type 1 thinking and people. Rarely, however, do Type 1's reveal themselves so blatantly. They prefer, at least, to appear more reasonable. But at heart, the Type 1 believes the world is a fixed objective fact and that he or she has the correct and only view of that reality. He or she believes the map to be the territory.

Most people like to believe they are not Type 1. They prefer to believe that they hold the more reasonable sounding position of 'My world is simply *my* or *a* or *one* of some five billion human worlds!' It follows from this position, which I will 'label' Type 2 thinking and people, that there are a myriad of different views, worlds and ideas – and that perhaps we can therefore entertain some of these different ways of world-making. The Type 2 thinker knows that you never have your hands directly on objective reality. You have your different interpretations of 'it', whatever 'it' or 'reality' may be. Your whole world is highly 'relative'. 'Relativism' and not 'absolutism' is the Bible or Koran.

This 'either/or' idea of Type 1 or 2 is a little too simplistic. Most people are mixtures of Type 1 and 2. And rather than thinking of the two positions as straightforward opposites, it makes more sense to see them as the two ends of a continuum scale:

Type 1   Type 2

0   5   10

And on such a scale, any individual has an overall score and then particular scores for specific topics. For example, you may see yourself as having an overall score of 5 or 6, and yet also recognise that your score may drop markedly on certain emotionally charged subjects. For example, when someone suggests that your political or moral viewpoints are nonsense – your reasonable Type 2 position of, at least, espoused relativism, may be bulldozed out of the way by a somewhat more dogmatic and certain Type 1 absolutism.

Recognising Type 1 and Type 2 Extremes

So, if most people are a blend of Type 1, 'My world is *the* world' and Type 2, 'My world is simply *my* or *a* or *one* world', what are the advantages and disadvantages of the two types? The following list states perhaps too clearly some of the differences. I have exaggerated the differences for the sake of initial clarity. These ideas will then be fine-tuned later on.

Type 1	Type 2
Resistant to change.	Open to change.
Uncomfortable with uncertainty, ambiguity, etc.	Sees uncertainty as a natural reflection of a fast-changing world.
Very good at seeing things from own point of view!	Able to see things from other people's perspectives.
Has predominantly one style of managing.	Has a range of management styles.
If other people do not perform, assumes that this reflects innate incompetence.	Views all people as having huge potential for development.
Slow to learn from mistakes and may have difficulty in acknowledging that they ever make mistakes!	Fast to learn from mistakes.
'Mistakes' are taboo. Keep a clean nose at all costs.	Knows that no mistakes means no development or innovation.
Slow to update their view – if at all.	Constantly updating their view or 'model of the world'.
Predictable if operating in a known and fixed environment (and successful).	Past patterns do not have to dictate what will be done in new situations. May not flourish in a routine environment.

Autocratic view of the world may well be reflected in leadership style.	Tends to adopt a more open and participative style.
Decisive (and can be decisively wrong!).	May take longer to come to a decision (or not make a decision at all!), but that decision-making process will have been more informed.
Tends to look at problems through a fixed historical mind-set.	Able to look at problems from several different angles – 'two heads are better than one'.
Problem-orientated.	'Opportunity-sensitive'.
'Yes . . . buts' and resists the new.	'Ands' and 'builds' and embraces the new.
May well have difficulty fitting into new teams unless he is boss or everybody agrees with him.	Flexible approach enables him to fit into new mixed teams.
Intolerant of disagreement and differences.	Uses disagreement to improve the quality of decision-making and sees differences as complementary.
Absolutely knows he is an excellent judge of character – and tends to select and promote people who fit his preferred stereotypes – rejects others.	Realises that all judgement is subjective and works hard to compensate for various factors that bias his view of others.

Given this list, it is little wonder that most people like to think of themselves as being closer to Type 2 than Type 1.

Recognising Yourself

And here is the bad news – practically all of us tend to see ourselves as Type 2 and simultaneously to see many, if not most, others as Type 1. In fact, the more you see yourself as Type 2, the more of a stuck, arrogant, Type 1 dinosaur, you may well be! The problem with many Type 1 thinkers is that they are so stuck that they don't even realise it! If anything, the more open and unstuck you are the more you see yourself as actually being more Type 1 than Type 2. This is because you realise just how difficult it is to remain open and relative in your approach. It's so easy to say that *my* world is mine and not *the* world – but living it is something quite different. This is especially so because although you may understand that your world is only one of many, as it is the only one you experience, you are therefore almost bound to take it as *the* world. In the same way that a calendar reform in 1752, which turned 2 September into 14 September, sent people off to Westminster demanding the return of those lost eleven days, it is so easy to mistake your world as being '*the* world'.[1]

What average score do you give yourself on the Type 1, Type 2 scale? You can mark it on page 18.

In fact, even understanding why it is that your world is *your* world and not *the* world is, in itself, difficult enough. The following discussion about how we see 'the world' will help explain why all of us never have our hands directly on 'out there' – but that each of us has our own unique construction of 'it'.

How You Perceive

Imagine some of the problems in building a domestic robot – a robot that wanders about your home tidying up, making beds, cooking meals and the like. Among the many design

problems to be solved there will be the central difficulty of
enabling the machine to *see*, in the sense of being able to
identify and recognise people, animals and other objects.
Knowing which is which is fairly critical for the smooth
running of domestic life. How might you go about this?

You might start by reading up about human vision. Early
on in your reading you would encounter the old 'homunculus' or 'little man theory' of perception. According to
this theory, the brain works like a miniature man who, like
a coastguard, keeps a look-out for what is going on. The
miniature man simply has to make sense of the images that
fall on the back of the eyes, the retinae. As the eyes invert
the image, the theoretical little man will have to be standing
on his head, so that the world appears to be the right way up!

Now hang on, you are saying, how does this precariously
balanced little man himself recognise what is presented by
those inverted images on the back of the eyes? Surely you
will have to suggest that inside the little man's head, there
is a still smaller man, this time standing the right way up,
who is looking at the images on the back of the homunculus'
eyes! And then again, a still smaller man, this time on his
head, and so on, *ad infinitum*.

The problem with this old 'passive' theory of perception
is that it never answers the question of how we actually
identify objects, recognise and understand our visual world.
(Obviously the same discussion and problems apply to
thinking about our other senses of smell, hearing, touch,
etc.) Instead it sets up the rather enchanting image of the
infinite number of ever smaller men, one inserted inside the
other, like a Russian doll. So enough of little men! What is
now clear is that the process of seeing is neither a passive
nor a simple process.

You will probably decide to design our domestic robot
along the same sort of lines that we humans work. And
you are able to see, to perceive everyday objects because
you have stored a 'model' or memory of those objects.
The process of perceiving therefore involves a 'matching'
of 'what is out there' to one of those models or memories.
Perception is an active matching process. And you are
only able to recognise the 'world' around you because of
the historical store of information that you have collected

about 'it'. In part, therefore you construe and create your own unique world.

No mind means no world. Or as George Orwell comments at the moment of a man's death: 'one mind less, one world less'.[2]

> Hitherto the poets and philosophers of science have used the vast expanse and duration of the universe as a pretext for reflections on the unimportance of man, forgetting that man with 'that enchanted loom, the brain' is precisely what transforms this immense electrical pulsation into 'light and color, shape and sound.'[3]

Now all this may sound a little extreme. Surely, you could well say, the whole process at least *seems* much simpler. I look up and see – that's all there is to it. There is no sensation of matching 'what is out there' to 'models of out there' stored in your brain. I agree. The process is so brilliantly executed that it operates effortlessly. But don't allow ease to belie the complexity and intelligence of the process. In order to realise for ourselves that we are at all times in the business of matching 'out there' with 'in here', let's try to capture, in the sense of make ourselves aware of, that matching process. We can do this by slowing down the matching and thus delaying the normally incredibly fast process of categorising and, thus, perceiving.

Now study Figure 2.1 and jot down below some of the things that you see in the image:

_____

_____

_____

_____

_____

Figure 2.1   The Hidden Man

Some people lock into one interpretation very quickly – especially if they have seen this image before. Others may see a variety of things – just a black and white pattern, a snowscape, islands, a lunar landscape or, say, certain animals. If you find that you are still open and not now 'stuck' with just one interpretation – *relish the moment* – you are behaving in a very Type 2 way. That is, like the innocent child, you are open to a range of alternatives. Experience has not yet forced you into accepting one interpretation of the world.

You may, however, find that you feel uncomfortable, even irritated, in not being able to categorise the image. 'What is this mess?' You may dislike the ambiguity and uncertainty presented by the pattern. All the same, the very fast matching process has been delayed and thus revealed. The complex array of neural signals sent from the retinae to the visual cortex only results in meaningful perception because of the historical information stored in our brains. You need your past to be able to begin to see and make sense of the world today. And already you may have guessed a problem. The way you see is very similar, in this respect, to the way you think. You are only able to understand today in terms of, and because of, the past. Yet, you also know that today is unlike yesterday. You inherit yesterday's patterns and need them to make sense of the present. These patterns are simultaneously essential and yet out of date.

If, by now, you have not seen the face of the bearded man, turn to page 27, and look at the image. Some see a religious figure, for example, Jesus Christ – others a cavalier figure. Then straight away turn back and look at the original image.

Most people find that once a model or memory has been suggested to try on for size, they instantly see the face of the bearded man or whoever. And they are often surprised that they didn't see it before, or that it took so long to see. The image now fits a small part of your historical grid of experience. You can now categorise the image by slotting it into an existing pattern, yet your eyes are receiving the same signal as when you simply saw a meaningless array of black and white patches.

Stuck in Your World

Now try to 'uncategorise' the image. Think and look afresh. Go back to the state of innocence of a few moments ago. Look at the image and *do not* see the face of the bearded man. And if you cannot do this, try harder! The chances are that you will be unsuccessful. Even though you accept, at least in theory that your world is simply your world, this awareness alone may not stop you being firmly stuck in just one view of the world. The price you often pay for experience is the development of one predominant and fixed way of looking at and thinking about the world.

There are some people who never see the face of the bearded man, even having seen the suggested guideline image. Don't worry if you are one of these people – you may just be very unstuck! However, so that you can appreciate the jump from the unstuck to the stuck, have a look at Figure 2.2.

As with the image of the bearded man, you start off in a state of innocence – exceptionally Type 2 – and then suddenly lock into the image of – a person lying down, or

Figure 2.2   What's This?

perhaps a field, or perhaps *a cow*! Once you've seen it, can you now ignore it? Stuck again?

To conclude, you don't passively see the world – you actively 'construe' it. You see, in part, what your past allows you to see. Therefore your world is unique and yet simultaneously limited (and enriched) in the light of your experience.

The sceptic may challenge the idea that people construe their worlds. He may say that surely the very degree of similarity between your world and mine must be proof that we are looking at the same one. As American psychologist, Robert Ornstein, points out:

> Our 'agreement' on reality is subject to common shared limitations that evolved to ensure the biological survival of the race. All humans agree on certain events only because we are all limited in our very structure as well as limited in our culture.[4]

In desperation the sceptic may say that there must be a scientific way of knowing reality. Surely, he says, this very book is made up of 'atoms' – and you can't get more objective than atoms! But when you ask the physicist to explain the nature of an atom, he replies that it:

Figure 3.2   The hidden man revealed

. . . is 'nothing but' a nucleus surrounded by a cloud of spinning electrons, which in turn are 'nothing but' eigenvalues in a probability function called the wave equation. What is 'an eigenvalue in a probability function called the wave equation'? Nothing but a model created by the conscious processes of the human mind to give meaning to certain experimental results in physics.[5]

In conclusion, we all construe our worlds, and although there may be much perceptual similarity, there is probably an infinite number of psychological worlds. The problem is that even realising that our worlds are not *the* world does not stop us being stuck in our own worlds. Thus, the next chapter.

References

1. Watts, A. *The Book*, Jonathan Cape, 1969, p. 79.
2. Orwell, G. *Decline of the English Murder (and other essays)*, Penguin, 1965.
3. Watts. Ibid. p. 139.
4. Ornstein, R. H. *The Psychology of Consciousness*, W. H. Freeman, 1972, p. 24.
5. Russell, P. *The Awakening Earth*, Arkana edition, 1988, p. 42.

CHAPTER THREE

Other People's Worlds

We all need to be good psychologists. That is, we need to be good at understanding other people's worlds. Why? Because each one of us is unique. Only by appreciating the unique worlds of others will we hold the key to, for example, communication, selling, marketing, motivation, delegation, and negotiation. Therefore we all need to be able to think and feel ourselves into other people's worlds.

If the bad news was that most people think they are Type 2s and believe that everybody else is stuck, here's some worse news still. You saw with the images of the 'bearded man' and the 'cow' that the perceptual system gets stuck with its primary interpretations, categories or grid of experience. The bad news now is *the perceptual system is in many ways comparatively flexible compared to the stuckness of the thinking and feeling system!*

If you can't get unstuck in looking at the bearded man and the cow – and, if the perceptual system is more flexible than the thinking and feeling systems – what hope is there of getting out of your own world and into other people's!

To witness the flexibility of the perceptual system, look at the images in Figures 3.1–5. What you may well find is that you can switch from one interpretation to another, and then, perhaps, back again, and so forth. (The young woman's chin becomes the old woman's nose.) The perceptual system is fast to explore and entertain different ways of putting the world together. This is less often the case when it comes to thinking and the emotions. When it comes to discussing

Figure 3.1   Young Girls - Old Women

Figure 3.2   Drabbit or Ruck?

Figure 3.3   Going Swimming or Having a Drink?[1]

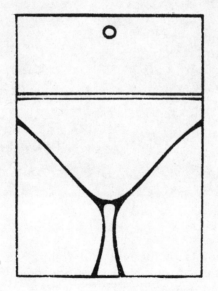

Figure 3.4   Au Revoir?

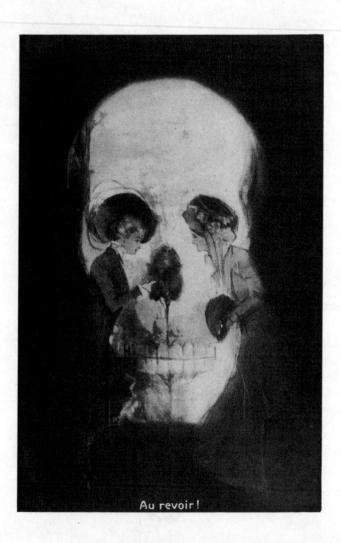

different 'points of thought and feeling', as opposed to, literally, different 'points of view', people often reveal far less preparedness and ability in getting into that other person's world.

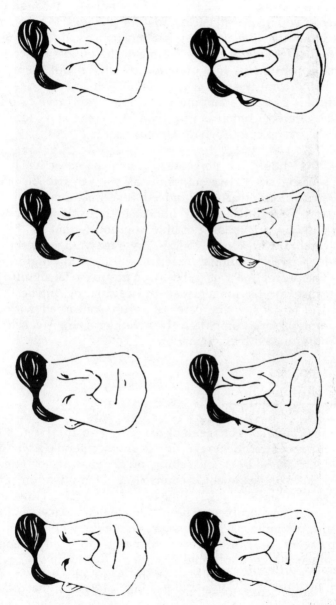

Figure 3.5 Man – Girl Figures

Figure 3.5 is especially fascinating. If you start from top left and read across as though reading a book, you will notice that you continue to see the face for a fair way through the series. If you then read backwards, starting with the woman, this alternative interpretation will stay for a considerable way through. Here we have an example of the mind's reluctance to let go of its first interpretation of what's 'out there'. In much the same way in a discussion, you may notice the seemingly excessive amount of evidence you have to offer (or be offered!) before an opinion is changed. As leading British psychologist Richard Gregory said:

> Why should the perceptual system be so active in seeking alternative solutions, as we see it to be in ambiguous situations? Indeed, it seems more active, and more intellectually honest in refusing to stick with one of many possible solutions, than is the cerebral cortex as a whole – if we may judge by the tenacity of irrational belief in politics and religion. The perceptual system has been of biological significance for far longer than the calculating intellect. The regions of the cerebral cortex concerned with thought are comparatively juvenile. They are self opinionated by comparison . . .[2]

The Ultimate Book

To most people, management teaching and thinking is all about the central idea of getting into other people's worlds. Read the latest book on selling or negotiating, or attend a seminar on leadership, counselling or motivation, and the same theme emerges time and time again. However, there may be a problem. These management concepts often provide a simple category system, where the whole world is then meant to fit into three or four slots. In reality, people are much more complicated.

Take selling for example. At the heart of many, if not most, approaches to selling lies the concept of 'features' and 'benefits'. A feature can be defined as a 'thing' or 'aspect' or 'neutral functional aspect' and a benefit is 'what interests or attracts' the potential buyer, or the 'positively perceived aspect'. The feature of an 'automatic gearbox' may be a positive benefit for one individual – indicating 'prestige, status, a free hand for using the car-phone'. On the other hand for another individual it may be the opposite – it is a turn-off, indicating 'unsporty, unexciting, old person's necessity'! No theory or rulebook can definitively predict what will turn one person on and yet at the same time turn another off. The way to find out is to climb into that person's head, heart and guts and experience his or her world as he or she does.

The same message of getting right inside another's skin is especially true, for all 'people' skills. From negotiators who defuse the explosive situation in a kidnap or hijack, through to successful military or management leaders, the core skill is the same – get into the other's world.

So here lies the weakness of many of the 'grand management theories' with over-simplistic categories concerning such diverse areas as motivation, selling, managing cross-cultural differences and the like. First of all, the theories tend to produce bland generalities of doubtful usefulness. Take motivation – to know that an individual will not produce much creative work if he or she is starving to death tells managers little they can use under normal working conditions. And even if the generality is of use, it may only be applicable to the individual who is a hundred per cent average – and that's a figment of the statistician's imagination.

Too harsh a criticism, the sceptic may argue. Surely, many theories give several character types, like different team membership, learning and leadership styles? A good point, but not good enough. For here is the second weakness. For Type 1 thinkers, you will need as many character types as there are people. Otherwise, as with stereotypes, they will fit people into categories that may not suit them at all well. Because humans dislike excessive complexity (and the world is infinitely complex) few people ever manage to use categories as a limited insight from which to explore – usually the categories harden into prison cells inside which misplaced victims languish indefinitely. However, these management theories can be of use, when applied in a Type 2 manner – more of this later.

Thus, human beings are too diverse and too complex to be subsumed within any framework. And such diversity and complexity probably helps to explain why it is that so many management theories, when applied too simply, fail to work in practice. In order to get through to another person, what one needs is not primarily another course, workshop, book or grand academic theory, but the ability to know that person's world. And unless he or she has written a very candid autobiography, there is only one way you are going to get that: by climbing right into that world. This is why effective managers (and parents, teachers, social workers) have to be good appreciators of other people's minds and hearts – in other words, psychologists.

So What's the Problem?

Five initial problems spring to mind when it comes to getting into other people's worlds. These are:

1. the problem of the problem,
2. excessive 'critical' listening,
3. content mismatch,
4. context mismatch, and
5. threat to your own point of view.

The Problem of the Problem

First of all, from the viewpoint of Type 1 thinkers, there is no problem, as their world is *the* world. This really is a problem, therefore! Secondly, a Type 2 thinker may underemphasise the difference between worlds. If we could literally try each other's heads on for size, so as to gain an appreciation of the uniqueness of another's world – it would be our most memorable experience. Each of us inhabits a unique and personal universe. Great literature can provide brilliant insight into the uniqueness of and the differences between worlds.

To obtain a sense of the uniqueness of your own and other people's worlds, you can capture a part of what your world looks like by filling in the grid at the end of the book. There are two copies of this grid, so that you and another person can fill it in and then compare worlds. It is in looking at the differences that you begin to appreciate the sensible arbitrariness of different people's worlds.

The grid will take some ten minutes to fill in. It will substantially increase your learning and enjoyment in reading the rest of the book, as it will help you gain insight into how you form your judgements about other people and what makes you 'tick'.

Mapping your own Unique World[3]

First of all, think of ten different people, each of whom you have known personally. Each should have made some lasting impression on you. For this reason, parent/s are often used. The people that you think of may be alive or now dead. All that matters is that you have known them and they have an influence, positive or otherwise, on you. Typical individuals include, as well as parents: brothers, sisters, girl/boyfriends, partners, work colleagues, old friends, school/college friends, other relatives, etc. Put the name of one next to each number. Simply jot down the name you use/d to call them.

Ten people who have made a lasting impression on you

1 _____

2 _____

3 _____

4 _____

5 _____

6 _____

7 _____

8 _____

9 _____

10 _____

Now look at the first three names, 1, 2 and 3 and ask yourself the question:

In what way are two of these alike and the other different?

You are looking for significant psychological differences,
and not simply superficial ones. So, for example, you might
say that two of the three are alike in that they are both
'good-humoured', whereas the other is somewhat 'sullen'.
These adjectives are more fundamental than simply saying
that two are tall and the other is short (unless, of course, you
find height a very important dimension through which you
make sense of the world). Don't try and constrain yourself
to logical opposites – 'happy, unhappy', etc. If you see two
as 'happy' and the other as 'pessimistic', that's fine.

Continue with the next three people, and then the following combination of people, as indicated on the example
grid. Don't worry if you can't fill in all ten combinations. Ten
is the ideal, seven or eight will do. Lastly, avoid repeating
the same dimension, for example 'extrovert – introvert' and
instead look for a new pair of adjectives.

Example Judgement Grid
(This is my own. I have added weightings of positive (+),
neutral (0), and negative (−). That is, if I liked the characteristic I weighted it '+', etc.)

1 2 3
laughs and is   serious
carefree
(+)   (−)
-------------------   ━━━━━━━━━━━━━━━━━   -------------------

4 5 6
thinks   feels and intuits
(+)   (+)
----------------- ——————————————— --------------------

7 8 9
social   selfish
conscience
(+)   (−)
----------------- ——————————————— --------------------

10 1 4
self-assured   self-doubting
(+)   (0)
----------------- ——————————————— --------------------

2 5 7
has a cause   causeless
(+)   (0)
-------------------- —————————— --------------------

3 6 8
enjoys thinking   dislikes thinking
(+)   (−)
----------------- ——————————————— --------------------

9 10 2
magical   mundane
(+)   (−)
-------------------- —————————— --------------------

3 4 9
high integrity   shifty
(+)   (−)
-------------------   ━━━━━━━━━━━━━━━━━   -------------------

1 5 8
aware   confused
(+)   (0)
-------------------   ━━━━━━━━━━━━━━━━━   -------------------

10 7 6
open heart   concealed heart
(+)   (0)
-------------------   ━━━━━━━━━━━━━━━━━   -------------------

Having completed the Judgement Grid, decide whether
you rate certain characteristics on it as positive, neutral or
negative. Be aware that psychological worlds do not follow
the world of logic – they are 'psycho-logical'. You may find
that you rate both of the characteristics in a particular
comparison in the same way – as for example I have done
for 'thinks/feels and intuits' in my own grid.

When comparing your grid with another, contrast both
the adjectives and the scoring of positive, neutral or negative. You will begin to get a sense of just how different others'
worlds are. (This is just a start; we will be making further use
of the grids later on.)

So, if you can acknowledge that others' worlds are radical-
ly different, you have successfully jumped the first hurdle.
Now comes the next obstacle to getting into that other
person's head, heart and guts – listening.

Creative Listening

You may consider yourself to be a good listener. However, this is often so only because we have a limited understanding of what it means to listen. To elaborate on this idea, a scale of listening competencies may help:

Critical listening   Creative listening

0   5   10

'jaw jealousy'
head chatter   a quiet mind

preparing what you
want to say next
while other is
talking

hearing and seeing   empathy
things from your   living in the other
point of view   person's head, heart
                                                      and guts

Much of the time, people operate at the 0, 1, 2, 3 level – because they are involved in a 'chat' type conversation. People, understandably, like to take an active part in the conversation. Jaws get jealous. We often interrupt each other.

Furthermore the supposed listener is often distracted by a fair degree of 'head chatter'. This is the noise that goes on in your head while someone else is talking. It takes two forms. The first is preparing your reply. People in Western society are particularly uncomfortable with periods of silence in a conversation. They therefore usually prepare their reply as the first speaker is making or winding up their point. The second form of head chatter, which is even more distracting to the act of listening, arises when the speaker

says something you strongly disagree with. It is as though
someone has dropped a match into a box of fireworks inside
your head – as all the rockets of disagreement ricochet
around your skull, the noise is such that you hear little, if
anything, of what follows.

Try, at a typical meeting, counting the number of
thoughts, whether relevant or irrelevant that come into your
mind while you listen to a presentation or point being made.
Just jot down a tick for each bit of head chatter. You may
decide that your mind is in mutiny. Most of us are habitual
judges of what others say. Of course, it is important to be
able to evaluate both people and the points they make. But
if the tendency gets to be a compulsion . . .[4]

Most people think of listening as what is, therefore,
described above as 'critical listening'. Critical listening is
to listen for what you agree and disagree with. It is to listen
and judge and prepare your point at the same time as the
other is talking. And as *a* style of listening it is very useful.
However, for many of us, it is the *only* style of listening. The
successful listener has the ability to move up and down the
scale as appropriate. If he needs really to listen, he can.

The listener, operating at 8, 9, 10, has stopped the jaw
jealousy and the head chatter – that is, he or she has managed to stop talking for a time and is beginning to get into
the other's head, heart and guts. However, there are new
obstacles at this stage.

Content Match – What Worlds Contain

If you were asked to sketch the past and present content
of your world, what might you draw? Part of the content's
picture might well contain family, work, other interests and
childhood details. What is certain is that no two worlds
would ever have exactly the same contents. Even identical
twins have different life experiences.

So, in trying to get into another's world, you may be
helped if you have similar backgrounds. However, this may
not always be the case. For example, if you start to relate an
experience, say a car accident, to someone who has had a
similar experience, he may keep absorbing what you say so

that it fits *his* experience and not yours. In other words, a close content match may result in you jumping to too many wrong conclusions about that other world, because of its apparent similarity to your own.

The lower the content match, therefore, the more imaginative and creative you need to be so as to be able to manufacture a sense of the contents of that other world. Effective communication is thus a highly imaginative skill. And even if you achieve a *content* match, there may not be a *context* match. This is the next hurdle.

Context Match – How you Construe and Represent Your World

Imagine you meet someone on a train, who, as it turns out, has a high content match with you. He does the same work as yourself and has almost identical interests. It would therefore seem that you have 'everything in common'. Shouldn't creative listening, in this case, be plain sailing?

As you have guessed, although you may find that you have a high content match with another person, you may still find it difficult to get on that person's *wavelength*. And 'wavelength' is the appropriate term.

As shown in your Judgement Grid, each of us lives in a world where the feel or context is unique. The context in the Judgement Grid was revealed in the weighted descriptions used to capture the ends of the scales. Your travelling companion may have a central way of looking at the world that looks like:

Conventional	Bizarre
(+)	(−)

You may share the same pair of contrasting characteristics except that the plus and minus are reversed! Equally, your companion's grid may feature a pair of characteristics which are central to his world-view, such as:

Political   Apolitical
(+)   (−)
-------------------- ———————————— --------------------

when this just isn't an issue for you at all. In other words
the comparison and all it may imply is simply not a feature
of your world.

Context therefore includes the different psychological
realities that we live in and the priorities within those
realities. To go back to the twins, even if they had remarkably
similar childhoods, they will very probably make sense of
their pasts in different, if not very different, ways.

Alongside this 'psychological context' there is the
'representational context'. The representational context
describes the manner in which you *internally design and
externally portray* – that is, communicate your world to
others. Some of us, for example, live in very *visual* worlds,
where we talk about 'seeing the big picture; I see what you
mean'. Others live in a more *tangible* world where we like to
'grapple with the problem; get to grips with the situation'.
Again some of us live in a more *emotionally* orientated world
where 'things feel right; my gut feeling tells me'. Lastly some
live in a *conceptual* world where it is a question of 'really
understanding the theory; understanding the underlying
assumptions', and the like.[5]

Any individual will represent his or her internal world,
both to himself – i.e. thought, and to others – i.e. communication with a *blend* of styles or contexts.

The effective communicator has the ability to listen creatively to the other and appreciate the content and context of
the other person's world – and then is able to communicate
so as to connect with that world(see Figure 3.6).

'Yes but', the sceptic chips in – 'that's manipulation'.
Notice that the word 'manipulation' is acting as a 'mini-
mind-set'. It, perhaps, carries a pejorative connotation by
suggesting getting another to do something against his will.
I use the word without that connotation. I would, however,
probably need to choose another word if I were talking with
a Type 1 sceptic! Effective communication requires a full
understanding and appreciation of the other person's world.

Figure 3.6   Getting into the Other's World

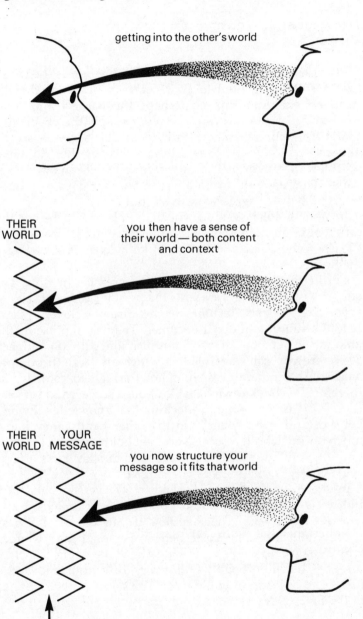

getting into the other's world

THEIR
WORLD

you then have a sense of
their world — both content
and context

THEIR   YOUR
WORLD   MESSAGE

you now structure your
message so it fits that world

GOOD FIT

What you then decide to communicate is then up to you.

Hot Planets: the Threat to Your Own Points of View

The last hurdle to getting into the other's world is the threat that may be presented to your centrally held, emotionally deep beliefs. And this is perhaps the hardest and most interesting barrier to overcome. Very simply the problem is that if we go round really getting into people's worlds, seeing and appreciating why they think and feel as they do, what will start to happen to our own central beliefs and points of view? True enough, to understand another does not mean that you have to agree with them, but . . .

Imagine a solar system, where the planets represent the different bodies of knowledge and experience that you have. Clearly some planets or bodies of knowledge will be larger than others.

Furthermore, certain planets are closer to the sun. The sun, in this analogy, represents the person's sense of self, or, if you like, the ego. Assume, for this case, the closer a planet is to the sun, the hotter it becomes. The heat represents the amount of personal or ego identification with the subject. Therefore you can have planets which are large through to small with temperatures from hot through to cold. I may therefore be very knowledgeable about a subject and yet very cool. If I sense someone is attacking that knowledge, I won't get 'hot under the collar'. On the other hand I may know much or little about a subject and yet hold my knowledge or opinion very hotly and so will respond quickly and perhaps aggressively if that view is challenged.

In the example shown in Figure 3.7, Person 1 is 'hot' but not very informed about politics, whereas Person 2 is cool and informed. What happens if they discuss politics? If they hold the same basic beliefs, Person 1 may wonder why Person 2 is so dispassionate about the subject. If they disagree, he will probably find it very difficult to take on the insights that Person 2 could offer. The same analysis applies to the topic of 'racism'.

Figure 3.7 Hot Planets

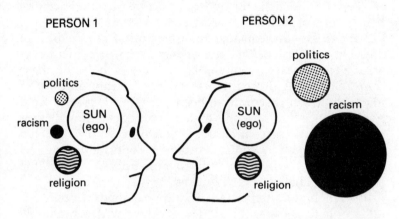

The style of any conversation on the topic of religion depends, again, whether or not they share the same kind of belief. If they disagree, we may find they either decide to drop the subject or that they avoid each other in the future.

Now, these hot or central 'planets' may create noise when you are trying to appreciate another's point of view. If you find that your world-view is being challenged in these central hot areas you may slip down the listening scale, towards critical listening – or not listening at all. Thus begins the 'dialogue of the deaf'.

You may want to jot down some of your 'hot' and 'warm' planets:

_____

_____

_____

_____

_____

_____

A disturbing thought for many who like to think that they are Type 2 thinkers is the question 'Do we own these central beliefs and outlooks – or are we the victims of them?' To explain this point, consider the question of where most of these hot central beliefs come from. What a coincidence, what a *co-incidence*, what similarity there is, between these core· beliefs and the particular society, culture and era of history into which you have been born. Furthermore, what a coincidence that so many with similar backgrounds agree with you in these central areas. You often know that you are right – in other words, full-blown Type 1 thinking. As Voltaire said, 'Opinion has caused more trouble on this little earth than plagues or earthquakes.'

In warm and hotter areas it may appear almost impossible for people to get into the worlds of others with whom they disagree. Furthermore it seems clear that many of these central opinions 'own' the people, rather than them owning the opinions.

'We are incredibly heedless in the formation of our beliefs, but find ourselves filled with an illicit passion for them when anyone proposes to rob us of their companionship.'[6]

To complete the trick, we so easily go on believing that we are exercising free will and logical thought over such areas – like the perfect clone which has been programmed to believe that it is a free-thinking and rational being. When you ask it the question 'Are you a clone?', naturally, it will answer, 'Of course not'. Are you a clone? Am I a clone?

This clone business is quite a problem. Many opine forth furiously without realising the ease with which opinions take over. When you have a warm or hot planet there are several effects on the way you view and think about your world.

Selective seeing

You tend to become highly selective of the evidence that supports your point of view and blind to contradictory evidence. Such sensitivity is well known to everyone. You get a new car and suddenly the roads appear over-flowing with the same model. It's as though they have been breeding overnight in back streets! You are reading a newspaper or book and come across a word you don't know. Over the next few days and months you come across the word with uncanny regularity. You are standing in a group at a party and the noise around you is 'babble, babble, babble'. Over the other side of the room someone mentions your name and you notice it at once. And you can probably think of numerous other examples – you are very fast to notice your own company's logo and advertising; if you are a professional proofreader, you may find it difficult to turn off and read a book for pleasure – your mind is still set for spelling and punctuation errors; if you have been trying to sell or buy property your life will be full of 'for sale' signs.

Such selective and sensitised seeing may even explain such oddities as why dogs look like their owners! I would hate to deny the folklore that suggests that people naturally select animals which look like them – or perhaps that the two grow alike in looks and mannerisms (see Figure 3.8). A simpler explanation lies in the idea that once your mind is set you will be quick to notice all supporting evidence. If you have just looked at a dog with very bushy eyebrows your mind will be set to notice the eyebrows of the owner. If you are watching a fat dog roll from side to side as it waddles down the street, you will be very sensitive to noticing any rolling movement whatsoever in the owner.

We notice what supports our expectations and ignore the rest, as classically demonstrated in:

and

We see what we expect to see and miss out the repeated words. In the same way, when Darwin arrived at Patagonia, the natives did not see his ship, the Beagle, but could immediately see the small boats used for landing. Small boats they knew, large sailing vessels they did not.

This tendency only to notice confirming evidence for an

Figure 3.8   Animals and Owners

Fig. 1 Fig. 2 Fig. 3 Fig. 4 Fig. 5 Fig. 6

Fig. 1 Fig. 2 Fig. 3 Fig. 4 Fig. 5 Fig. 6

Fig. 1 Fig. 2 Fig. 3 Fig. 4 Fig. 5 Fig. 6

Siné

idea or suggestion goes a long way towards explaining the faith some people show in popular astrology. The individual perceives the world so as to fit the prophecy. Likewise, this confirmatory bias explains many of life's supposed coincidences.

It may be more accurate to say that once a hot attitude is formed, you don't simply notice what supports your view, but that you create evidence and 'facts' to support it. What is a 'fact' in one person's world may simply not be a 'fact' in another's. Take political opinion. Give a Tory and a Marxist the same newspaper to read. When you discuss the news with them afterwards you get the impression that they must have read two completely different newspapers.

New information or evidence that goes counter to an existing opinion may not influence that view at all. In fact, it may harden that view. For example, take the issue of whether or not capital punishment is an effective deterrent. Now present as rounded, balanced and informed a case as possible, stating all the pros and cons, to two groups of equally intelligent adults. However, one of those groups favours the death penalty and the other is against it. You might expect that both groups would become more moderate in their points of view once exposed to challenging evidence, some of which refutes both their existing points of view. Research, however, suggests the opposite.[7] People become *more* polarised and extreme in their existing points of view. In other words, where people have made up their minds, well-balanced arguments and further research often make their existing convictions even more rather than less concrete and sure.

One ingenious experiment involved a psychologist who learnt by heart a speech which had originally been given by Franklin Roosevelt concerning the New Deal Programme. He then gave the speech to his students:

> . . . it was found that the Democrats had heard a speech favouring the New Deal; and they could cite statements to support this assertion. Conversely, the Republicans had heard a speech attacking the New Deal, and they too could quote evidence for their view. Each had heard what he had wanted to hear, or what was compatible with his pre existing bias.[8]

Furthermore, when the students were requestioned three weeks later, an even greater distortion had taken place in favour of their existing mind-sets.

> . . . it is inaccurate and misleading to say that different people have different 'attitudes' concerning the same 'thing'. For the 'thing' simply is *not* the same for different people whether the 'thing' is a football game, a presidential candidate, Communism or spinach. We do not simply 'react to' a happening or to some impingement from the environment in a determined way . . . We behave according to what we bring to the occasion, and what each of us brings to the occasion is more or less unique.[9]

Rationalising

Not only do we adjust the world to suit our attitudes but we then tend to rationalise rather than reason in our thinking. In other words, thinking is often used as a tool to substantiate our point of view, rather than as a tool of inquiry and possible challenge. So when you rationalise you simply use and abuse reason to reach whatever is your predetermined destination. Thinking becomes crooked.[10]

> Reason is a tool, and a tool that is wielded in the service of assumptions, beliefs, and needs which are not themselves subject to reason.[11]

You could say that we humans suffer from illusions of rationality!

Our actual ability to reason and judge the quality of reasoning of another diminishes if the conclusions of such crooked reasoning fit our deep or hot beliefs. If we feel strongly about the subject under discussion we are much more likely to accept the conclusion '. . . with little regard for the correctness or incorrectness of inferences involved'.[12] For example, those who are racially prejudiced show more distortion in their reasoning on racial issues than those who are not racially prejudiced.[13]

Don't Attack Hot Planets!

Any confrontation or attack on one of the hotter central planets, is often experienced as an attack on oneself. A person's sense of identity is often inextricably intertwined with his central beliefs. And when you feel attacked, you often find that your attitudes harden, rather than open up for possible revision. This is why referring to groups whose beliefs you strongly disagree with as psychopaths and maniacs does little to change opinions. No matter how extraordinary and perhaps abhorrent another's point of view is, each and every time you exclaim that you cannot understand such people – this should act to remind you of how easy it is to be stuck in your own world and not appreciate the psychological reality of other worlds.

There is, therefore, a straightforward piece of advice when it comes to trying to change another person's central and hotly held belief – *don't argue against their position* – as they will tend to feel threatened and harden in their attitude. You are more likely to have an impact on their opinion if you listen, if you try to climb right into their world.[14]

The Clone Test

And, as you may have guessed, if you want to ensure that you are not a clone, what can you do? You might suggest that you could keep an open mind – the problem will be similar to trying *not* to see the face of the bearded man. You might recommend exposing yourself to points of view that challenge your own central beliefs. Granted this may have some effect, but the difficulty may be that you will be filtering all the counter-evidence through your selective grid of experience and then manipulating the remnants through a process of rationalisation.

Mind you, this is probably one of the best ways of ensuring you are not a clone. Keep exposing yourself to opinions that you disagree with – which is the opposite of what most of us do – 'birds of a feather flock together' – at the club, the pub, the conference. And one way to carry on checking that you are not a clone is to practise creative listening with those that you disagree with.

And here lies the real challenge. If you really climb right into another person's world and see and feel it from their point of view, what might happen to your originally differing viewpoint? Yes, you might change your mind. And that's what free-thinking individuals do. I think it was Voltaire who said: 'Doubt is uncomfortable. Certainty is ridiculous.'[15] So, to understand fully another person's point of view will sometimes require you to take on board values and outlooks that directly challenge your own central and dearly held beliefs. In doing this you will truly get into that other world – and *simultaneously* you will be taking the clone test, because you are opening yourself up to perspectives and values that may change your viewpoint. But there again . . .

Try counting the number of letter F's in the sentence in italics below. 'F' here means the letter 'F', capital or lower case 'f'. There is no trick.

Finished files are the result of years of scientific research combined with experience of many years.

Number of 'F's' counted   ——————

Now, simply jot down your percentage certainty. For example if you are absolutely certain you might jot down '100 per cent' or if you are fairly sure '70 per cent' etc.

Percentage certainty   ——————

This little teaser results in a fair few people saying there are somewhere between one and five 'F's'. The most common reply is that there are simply three. You then find that many people are prepared to say that they are 100 per cent certain about their reply – despite having gone along with the idea of being a Type 2 thinker who agrees that whereas doubt is uncomfortable, *certainty is ridiculous.*

The reason why many people say there are not six 'F's' is because their grid of experience screens out the 'F's' in the word 'of', that itself appears three times. The 'F' in 'of' is pronounced more as a 'v', as in 'ov', rather than an 'f' as in 'if'. So many of us scan for a sound and thus miss three of the target letters, as these have a different sound from the one we are looking for.

By the way, congratulations, if you spotted all six 'F's', first time round (that is assuming you haven't seen the game before). Mind you, are you sure there are only six? Absolutely, that is?

Bear in mind, that in the same way that many people see fewer than the six target letters, all of us, most of the time are living with our own highly tuned grids of experience that only pick up desired information. Our whole lives are a massive version of the 'F's' game. Again, what a surprise that there are some five billion people in the world who agree with themselves, and yet so often disagree with others! As *Time* magazine pointed out:

> Kings in the fifteenth century were known to have held their summit meetings in the middle of a bridge. The two sovereigns did their talking through a stout oak lattice set up between them, like the prison grate during visitor's hours. That way, neither could kidnap the other.
>
> Ronald Reagan and Mikhail Gorbachev talked in Geneva through more complex lattices. They sat by the fire in the Château Fleur d'Eau and interpreted the world for each other through their distinctive mental grids – different societies, different interests, minds formed by different histories. Walter Lippmann wrote, 'We are all captives of the pictures in our head – our belief that the world we experience is the world that really exists.' Reagan explained America to Gorbachev. Gorbachev explained the Soviet Union to Reagan. Neither man was moved to defect as a result of the education.[16]

Try the clone test – try creative listening. You may even find yourself changing your mind – time and time again. What chaos! But, if life were certain, would it be at all enjoyable?

Other People's Worlds in Action

No matter what area of people management you focus on, be it customer care or sales techniques, the ability that differentiates the successful from the unsuccessful individual and organisation is the ability to decentre – to get out of your own or your company's world and into the other's head, heart and guts.

In the case of customers, you do this by staying as close to them as possible and asking them, again and again what it is they want. Furthermore you structure your organisation so that you hear and act upon what your customers say. For example, in 1981, SAS, the Scandinavian Airline, made an $8 million loss. Jan Carlzon became President and that loss changed to a gross profit of $71 million on sales of $2 billion in just over a year. And the key behind his success? Looking after the customer at each and every point of contact with the organisation. Supposedly he did this, in part, by turning the organisational chart on its head, thus stressing the paramount importance of frontline people – that is, those people who have critical contact with the customer.

But, the sceptic may say, different customers want different things. This is 'marketing mania'.[17] We can't be all things to all people – not unless we can design the perfect chameleon product, that is 'self-marketing'. This is a sound point and justifies the distinction between the 'design' phase and 'delivery' phases of running an organisation.

In the design phase you are up against the problem that every person's world is different. For example, in the world of computer software, I can have a unique program written to suit me totally. It will, however, be expensive. On the other hand, I can go out and buy an existing software package that does what I mostly need – and probably a considerable amount more that I don't need but that other users do. The package may therefore suit me fairly well and will be a fraction of the cost.

So you can represent one person's world and needs as shown in Figure 3.9(a),and another's as in Figure 3.9(b). The indented points represent actual needs.

If we combine the two profiles (Figure 3.9(c)), there is a

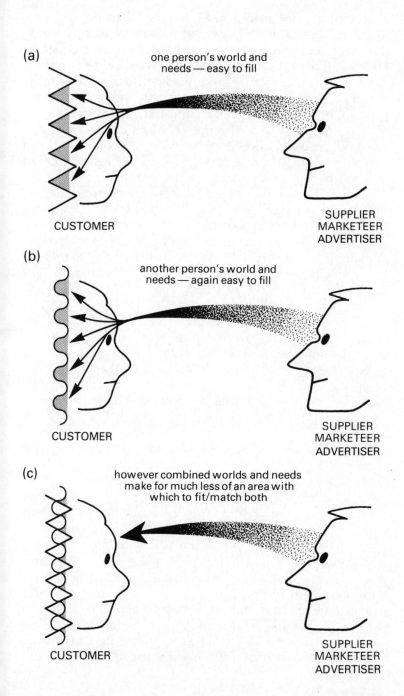

(a) one person's world and needs — easy to fill

CUSTOMER

SUPPLIER
MARKETEER
ADVERTISER

(b) another person's world and needs — again easy to fill

CUSTOMER

SUPPLIER
MARKETEER
ADVERTISER

(c) however combined worlds and needs make for much less of an area with which to fit/match both

CUSTOMER

SUPPLIER
MARKETEER
ADVERTISER

decreased area of shared need. Successful marketing aims to tap the most effective ways of measuring and maximising these common areas. Therefore marketeers are usually forced to trade off price against need(s), or rather perceived need(s). This is also true for any advertising campaign. As you are aiming for a fair few target people, you will hit some, partially hit others, miss many and lastly turn some others off. The Marlboro advertisements, I assume, must appeal to some people. However, personally, I have never been attracted to the idea of lurching around the Arizona desert as a full-blown cowboy surrounded by the aroma of horse manure and tobacco smoke. This advertisement has always been of considerable help in quitting smoking! It turns me off, but presumably it is attractive to others.

So, in the design phase, say with product development, marketing and advertising, you are usually trying to find the highest common denominator for your target group. This must limit the degree to which you can personalise any product or service.

In certain product and service areas, however, this assumed wisdom may be changing. It is becoming increasingly common to design, for example, software, so that it bespokes itself to the unique needs of the user. Those companies which seriously consider the idea of the mass 'self-marketing' or tailoring product, may begin to find a way around the old price/ need trade-off.

Whereas in design and manufacture there are these constraints, they are reduced or evaporate completely when it comes to the 'distribution' stage of the service or product. (Experience may lead you to doubt this – having had numerous American shop assistants all tell you 'Have a nice day', each with identical expressions. This is a perfect example of a failure to adapt, where, in fact, there is full scope for adapting. There are no design limitations here whatsoever.)

Within the bounds of integrity, there are a thousand ways of presenting and personalising a product or service at this later 'distribution'stage. By knowing the buyer's world you can tailor your approach completely. I recall when working in Saudi Arabia a problem experienced by some new expatriate car sales outlet managers. A new car would arrive from the factory covered with protective grease and paper. Understandably, these new managers would have the cars cleaned up for sale – as they used to do in Britain. Some Arab purchasers, however, did not want 'clean' cars. Having a car covered in grease and protective paper was a clear statement that they had just bought a new car!

Your 'distribution', be it selling through to post-sale customer care, allows for a unique appreciation and response to other people's worlds.

You may want to think through your customers, external and internal. You may then want to consider whether you can provide some additional unique personalisation – more so than you are doing currently. There is often much more scope for such unique tailoring in the distribution phase than you normally assume.

External customers

1 _____

2 _____

3 _____

4 _____

5 _____

6 _____

7 _____

8 _____

9 _____

10 _____

What else can you do to personalise the service or product?

_____

_____

_____

_____

Internal customers

1 _____

2 _____

3 _____

4 _____

5 _____

6 _____

7 _____

8 _____

9 _____

10 _____

Again, how can you make the service/product more personalised?

_____

_____

‑‑‑‑‑‑‑‑

Do it Or . . .

The ability to climb out of our own world and into others is the key to development from childhood to adulthood. Supposedly, as you mature, you increase in your ability to decentre. Successful companies always have decentred. However, many a successful company, like some very old people, may regress and begin to view the world exclusively from their own point of view. From this perspective they begin to wonder what is the matter with the world – 'what are they complaining about'. Such companies may be right to reminisce about the 'good old days', when there were 'punters galore'. People and companies with grids of experience that are out of date or out of touch with those they wish to serve will never see good days again.

If you want to ensure that you never become an unthinking clone and that your organisation doesn't become companycentric, *simply(!)* get into other people's worlds. It's difficult and rewarding.

References

1. I originally saw this image in: Davidoff, J. B. *Differences in Visual Perception*, Crosby Lockwood Staples, 1975, p.196.
2. Gregory, R. L. *Eye and Brain*, World University Library, second edition, 1972, pp.223–224.
3. This section on Judgement Grids, along with a central theme throughout *The Dinosaur Strain* of our worlds being, in part, of our making, owes much, if not everything to the work of: Kelly, G. A. *The Psychology of Personal Constructs*, vols. 1 & 2, Norton, 1955.

An excellent introduction to Construct Theory is Bannister, D. & Fransella, F. *Inquiring Man*, Penguin, 1971.

4. I strongly recommend the work of Dr Rachel Pinney, whose booklet, *Creative Listening* can be obtained from:
    Children's Hours Trust,
    28, Wallace House,
    Caledonian Road,
    London N7 8TL.
    Tel: (01) 609 5568
    Her work applies to children and adults alike.

5. Neuro-Linguistic Programming (NLP) studies the different contexts people inhabit. Don't be put off by the name! And although NLP may seem to be geared towards psychotherapy, it is applicable in both business and private life.
    See, for example, Bandler, R. & Grinder, J. *Frogs into Princes*, Real People Press, 1979.

6. James Harvey Robinson

7. Lord, C. G., Ross, L. & Lepper, M. R. 'Biased assimilation and attitude polarization: the effects of prior theories on subsequently considered evidence.' *Journal of Personality and Social Psychology*, 1979, Vol. 37, No. 11, pp.2098–2109.

8. Stagner, R. *Psychological Aspect of International Conflict*, Brooks/Cole, 1967, p.159.

9. Hastorf, A. H. & Cantril, H. 'They saw a game: a case study.' *Journal of Abnormal and Social Psychology*, Vol. 49, Jan, 1954, p.133.

10. For an excellent insight into reasonable sounding but illogical thinking see: Thouless, R. H. *Straight and Crooked Thinking*, Pan, 1974.

11. Tart, C. T. 'States of consciousness and state-specific sciences.' in *The Nature of Human Consciousness*, Ornstein, R. E. (Ed.), W. H. Freeman, 1973, p.59.

12. Morgan, J. J. B. & Morton, J. T. 'The distortion of syllogistic reasoning produced by personal convictions.' *Journal of Social Psychology*, 1944, 20, p.39. And see, Oakhill, J. V. & Johnson-Laird, P. N. 'The effects of belief on the spontaneous production of syllogistic conclusions.' *Quarterly Journal of Experimental Psychology*, 1985, 37A, pp. 553–569.

13. Combs, A. W., Richards, A. H. & Richards, F. *Perceptual Psychology*, Harper & Row, 1976, p.140.

14. Pinney. Ibid.

15. I don't know and would very much like to.

16. *Time* magazine, article entitled 'Behind Closed Doors' by Lance Morrow, 2nd December, 1985, p.11.

17. Levitt, T.'Marketing Myopia.' HBR Classic, *Harvard Business Review*, September–October 1975, p.180.

CHAPTER FOUR

Getting to Know You

The ability to judge another accurately has long been a critical survival skill. If you thought that the tall red-haired man was friendly – and he wasn't . . . Today, the same skill is key, not so much for physical survival, but for success as a social and work animal. In recruitment, selection, selling, negotiating, leading, communicating, deciding who to do business with – your judgement is your main strength or Achilles heel.

And, it's probably true to say most of us think of ourselves as good judges of character. Practically everyone does. And, in turn, we probably know many other people (besides ourselves!) whose judgement of character is, at best, faulty.

So far we have concentrated on the importance and difficulty of getting into other people's worlds. We have focused on the importance of creative listening, matching with the content and context of the other person. We have considered the difficulties of creative listening in 'hot areas'. In this chapter, we will consider some of the biasing mechanisms which give us a potentially inaccurate view of another person.

Prisons of the Mind

For the sake of clarity let me somewhat over-boldly state the theme of this chapter:

Many of us rarely get to know other people.
We only 'meet' the stereotypes we already hold of others.

In other words, we have pre-made pigeon-holes, into which
we slot the myriad of different people we meet. And there
they remain, imprisoned. Whereas there are some five billion
people in the world, we probably run around with less
than, perhaps, a couple of dozen primary stereotypes or
pigeon-holes in our minds. The infinite variety of humankind
is twisted and distorted so as to fit this very limited number of
prisons of our mind. In doing this, we misjudge others, fail to
get to know them and often do the other person a disservice
by assuming things about them which are, alone, of our own
making and have little or nothing to do with them.

We prejudge people all the time and force them into our
pigeon-holes. And it is extraordinary the extent to which we
will go beyond the very limited amount of information that we
usually have about someone when we first meet. For example,
when one Briton meets another, he may have an immediate
sense of:

- the part of the country the other is from,
- their background,
- type of education,
- 'class' and job, right the way through to that person's
  political leanings.

These impressions may be accurate – or hugely out. How
can we check?

If you ask many an English person for his or her stereotype
of an 'American' you often get back – 'loud, check trousers,
over-friendly'. So there go 250 million people – all sucked
into one pigeon-hole!

Prejudgements

So why do we prejudge other people? Well, it gives us a
degree of predictability, a pattern on which to model our
behaviour towards them, so as to give some form of instant
relationship. We do this because the human world is infinitely
complex. To help cope with this complexity we develop the

idea of 'groups of things' or 'categories' or, in the case of people, 'stereotypes' and 'pigeon-holes'. We have categories for things (chairs, tables, rooms) and people (Americans, Italians, chartered accountants, punks, etc.).

We can be said to prejudge another when we:

1. accept the existence of a group or category of people; and
2. assume that this category implies something (i.e. fat people are jolly, red-haired people are quick-tempered, gays are . . . etc.); and
3. assume that the person we are now meeting fits the category, which in turn implies he/she has the characteristic(s) associated with it and, in turn,
4. fail to explore and appreciate the uniqueness of that person.

Now the sceptic might well ask, 'What if my beliefs about the group are right in the first place?' Sounds a bit Type 1 – my world is *the only* world. And it may well be that many of us do become Type 1 thinkers when it comes to judging other people. This ability is so important, that few of us dare consider that we might not be as good as we would like to think.

So, what about this point that our beliefs about a group could be right – assuming that we are not just being stuck? Well it's actually a little more complicated than that. As an example, let's look at the way we treat an everyday object – a chair. Chairs are a group of objects that have certain things in common – we can sit on them and they look alike in several ways. If someone asked you how many legs chairs have, you might initially reply that the answer is obvious – chairs have four legs. However, with a little more reflection you might begin to doubt this. There are probably things you would regard as chairs which have only three legs or only one (such as swivel chairs). So in the end we can only say that *most* chairs have four legs. This means that it is likely that the chair nearest you at the moment has four legs *but it is certainly not necessarily the case.*

Now with groups of people the situation is far more complex. We can say that we feel it is likely that 'young people' are 'rebellious' but unless we know every young

person in the world we cannot be anywhere near sure that
they are. And, of course, the point is that no one knows
every young person. Everyone who says that young people
are rebellious or that 'women' are 'caring' really means that
they think it *likely* that all, or at least many, are that way. So
our beliefs about people are no more than guesswork.

Where Do Our Beliefs About Each Other
Come From?

This said, you may still feel that you can be fairly sure
that certain 'groups' have certain characteristics and that
you can therefore predict with a degree of certainty what an
apparent member of that 'group' is or will be like. Well, let's
look at where our beliefs about a group of people come from.
Some of our beliefs are held by many people in our society.
For example, in Britain, there is the belief that 'Scots are big
drinkers'. This belief is part of the fabric of our society, and
it is passed on to all of us by many sources – our families, our
schools, newspapers, television, etc. Other beliefs we create
for ourselves. You may notice an apparent link between a
group of people and a certain type of behaviour. For instance,
the bad behaviour of a small section of people may stick
out in your mind. Because the images of this behaviour are
quite vivid in your memory, there may be an overwhelming
temptation to generalise.

   Now, whether your belief was held by people before
you were born and then passed on to you, or whether you
formed it yourself on the basis of direct or indirect (hearsay)
experience with some members of the supposed group, the
conclusion is the same: you are making a generalisation about
the group and you cannot be at all sure that this generalisation
can be applied to any or all of its members.

There Must Be a Kernel of Truth

At this point the sceptic becomes exasperated and exclaims,
'But, if there were no truth in the beliefs we hold about

groups, surely these beliefs would eventually go away?'
Well, not necessarily. When we believe that people have a
particular characteristic we look out for it in them – it's a
classic mind-set, whereby you notice what you are interested
in or expecting to see. As a result, as with evidence that
goes against our hot planets, we may miss, ignore or explain
away many of the occasions on which they do not act in the
way we expect them to. That is, our beliefs may persevere in
spite of the weakness or absence of evidence for them and
the overwhelming evidence against them. And as with all
mind-sets, we are not even aware that this selective seeing is
going on – 'How many F's in the following sentence . . .'

Expectations Turn 'Real'

Furthermore, the beliefs can actually create a 'reality'. If we
all believe a group of people to have a particular characteristic, then that 'group' may also come to label itself as having it.
Thus, if everyone believes Scots to be big drinkers, they may
come to see themselves as such. Consequently many Scots
may drink heavily in order to confirm the image they have
of themselves. In this way the beliefs become self-fulfilling
prophecies. More about these prophecies shortly.

I've Got to Hate Someone

Another reason why false beliefs do not simply go away is
because they sometimes serve a deep emotional purpose. For
example, it may help us cope with our own problems and internal conflicts to blame others. This is called 'scapegoating'.
It simply means that we make a person or group of people
the 'scapegoats' of our troubles. This can happen with whole
societies. That is, a whole society can use another group of
people as scapegoats for their own problems. For example,
whites might blame blacks or punks for a whole range of
social problems that may have little, if anything, to do with
them, and that may have everything to do with the emotional
problems of those holding these views. Such scapegoating
can obviously create horrendous problems, as seen in Nazi
behaviour towards the Jews during the Second World War.

Can I Overcome My Prejudices?

So does this mean that we should try and drop all the beliefs that we have about 'groups'? Well, in practice this would be very difficult to do. The beliefs that you develop as a result of your own experience with just a few members of a group may be quite cool, meaning they are easily available for inspection and change. You only need ask yourself whether you really have the evidence you need to make the sort of generalisation you are making – and the answer is usually 'No!' You can also try to notice each and every time you meet someone whom you feel should belong to a particular group who, as you get to know them, does not conform to your expectations. Be brave, try to prove yourself wrong. Only Type 1's have to be right all the time.

However, as mentioned earlier, many of our beliefs about other groups are shared with many other people. They become part of our social reality – that is they become accepted as real and definite by practically everyone around us. 'Men are . . .'; 'women are . . .' etc. And if practically everyone accepts a belief then it is very difficult for any individual to challenge it – the view seems obviously true and he or she will be constantly bombarded with the view held by the vast majority. These views are therefore quite central and may be emotionally hot, as they are tied up with the individual's sense of self. That is we partly define who we feel and think we are in reference to others and other groups, some of whom we don't like to associate with. If such central views are challenged we become uncomfortable and usually defensive.

The same defensive strategy will usually occur if we are challenged about those beliefs that serve some scapegoating purpose. It is in this area that we are probably at our least aware and are most Type 1. We need to remember that whenever we really know that we are right in our judgement, and not prejudiced at all, we must to watch out!

Only Bigots Say They Have No Prejudices

One first step to becoming a more accurate judge of others is to get some sense of prejudgements you make, that is prejudices you hold. *And we all have prejudices* – with the exception of Type 1 thinkers, of course!

Most self-aware people have a sense of some of their prejudices. However you cannot overemphasise the influence of family, education, peer group, media and culture on the formation of the child's view of the world and people generally. 'Natural' values, standards and attitudes, which we may subsequently see as 'common sense' may therefore remain unnoticed and go unchallenged. And all of us can fall prey to these very deep prejudices – and they may even influence our most noble attempts at objectivity. For example, in the area of racial prejudice and the scientific method:

> . . . the conclusions investigators have reached about whether Negroes are or are not innately inferior to whites in intelligence can be predicted from biographical and demographic data about the investigators . . .[1] Taken together these biographical data would seem to indicate that the investigators whose research was categorized as concluding that Negroes are innately inferior intellectually came from higher socio-economic backgrounds.[2]

We are constantly bombarded with stereotypes. For example, one analysis of six leading marriage and family textbooks concludes:

> The active, aggressive male was depicted as normal; the woman with high sexual drive was a 'nymphomaniac', needed 'psychiatric attention', and/or 'endangered her marriage' with her demands. Turning to sex roles, the male was the 'selector' in the courtship, and 'status bestower' in marriage. Traditional homemaker/breadwinner roles were upheld as natural,

proper, and expedient; women should sacrifice
'over-emancipation' if it threatened to weaken the
institution of marriage.[3]

Children's literature may also carry this same type of prejudice. Of 2,760 stories studied, the following image emerged.
'Boys . . . were more clever than girls by a four to one ratio.
They were more heroic (ratio 4:1) – e.g., saving others from
fires, stampedes, storms and rampaging buffalo.'[4] However,
there is evidence that the bias is reducing.[5] Lastly the same
bias is easily detected in humour and jokes:

> . . . over 1,000 jokes from the years 1947–48, 1957–58,
> and 1967–68 were analysed. There was six times as
> much anti-women as anti-men humor, with over 30
> per cent of all the jokes analysed being anti-women.
> Incongruously, women were shown as being dumb
> and incompetent, yet dominating and exploitative of
> men.[6]

The images and questions which follow, based on a prejudice
awareness increasing package I developed[7], will help you
gain a deeper insight into various prejudices that affect
your judgement. Insight will be achieved, that is, unless you
want to out guess each question and so attempt to conceal
your prejudices! As you look at each picture, jot down your
first reaction, your gut feel, without reflecting on what you
'should' put down or referring back to any previous image
or answer.

Figure 4.1 Newspapers

Who reads which newspaper?
(If you feel you would rather specify a different news-paper/newspapers, please do so.)

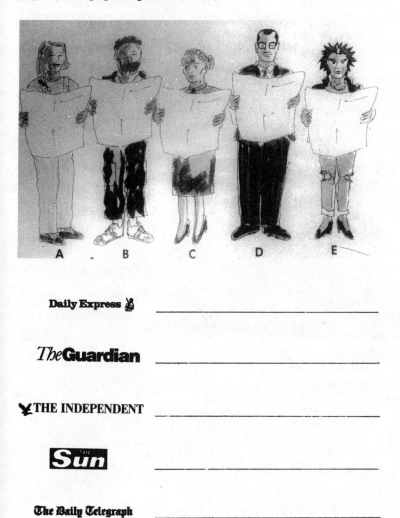

Daily Express _____

*The***Guardian** _____

THE INDEPENDENT _____

Sun _____

The Daily Telegraph _____

Figure 4.2   The Courtroom (a)

What might the charge well be?

....

....

Guilty or not guilty?

....

If guilty, what sentence?

....

Figure 4.3   Travelling Companions

If you were on a long journey, which of these people would you rather sit next to? Rank them in order of preference.

1st choice   ....

2nd choice   ....

3rd choice   ....

4th choice   ....

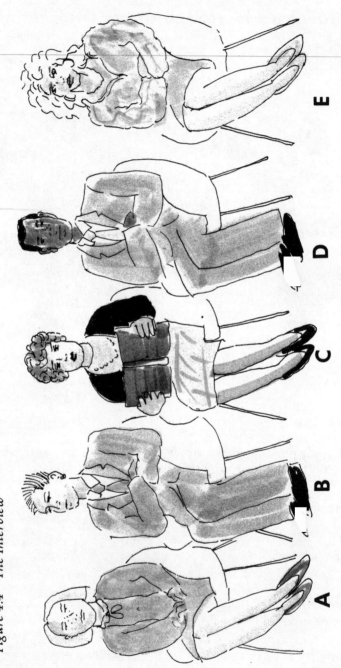

Figure 4.4   The Interview

A   B   C   D   E

What qualifications would you guess each person to have?

A ....

B ....

C ....

D ....

E ....

Do you feel your organisation would recruit this individual?

A ....

B ....

C ....

D ....

E ....

If yes, for what job?

A ....

B ....

C ....

D ....

E ....

Figure 4.5   Personality

Please jot down three or four adjectives that you imagine
describe the characters of these people.

a ....

....

b ....

....

c...

....

Figure 4.6   Man at Desk (a)

What job level would you guess this person to be at?

....

Figure 4.7   Paperwork

What jobs might these people do?

....

....

....

....

....

Figure 4.8   The Courtroom (b)

What might the charge well be?

....

....

....

Guilty or not guilty?

....

If guilty, what sentence?

....

Figure 4.9   Man at Desk (b)

What job level would you guess this person to be at?

....

Now, have a look at your replies. Is there any discernible pattern to them? Are you seeing men or women in a more favourable light? Is there any telling difference in your descriptions of whites and non-whites? Do you see the man and woman in the dock of the courtroom in the same or different lights? Does the wheelchair change your impression of the man working at the computer? Can you now begin to identify some of the primary positive and negative stereotypes that you hold?

Halos and Horns

In the light of the above and because of your own insight, list all the categories or stereotypes that you are aware of – positive and negative ones. Positives will result in you tending to see those people with a halo, and negatives – with horns!

Positive – halos	Negative – horns

Now add to the list all the other characteristics about people that turn you 'on' and 'off' – for example, types of dress, accent and manner. Obviously avoid the things that turn everyone off – people who are rude, drunk, etc. And, if possible, use the word that best captures your gut feeling – if you don't like homosexuals and you normally call them 'queers', call them queers. By the way, many people notice that their list of 'turn-offs' is much, much longer than the list of 'turn-ons'! What might this suggest?

Initially, some people may feel that the airing of these prejudices is not a good idea. Furthermore using derogatory words to describe groups you don't like may also seem at odds with the notion of reducing prejudice. The opposite is probably the case for most of us. The growth of public awareness about prejudice, along with the growth of public bodies whose job it is to try and ensure fair opportunities for all 'groups', results in much prejudice and associated language being driven underground, at least most of the time – for example, just watch an all-male or all-female group after a few drinks and notice how various comments and jokes reflect an underlying sexism. Even if prejudice is driven underground, it is still there, affecting our outlook and behaviour.

By making our own prejudices explicit, many of us begin to recognise a conflict between the image we like to hold of ourselves as fair and intelligent human beings, on the one hand, and on the other, our tendency to hold views about others that are unfair and unthinking. The creation of such conflict, or 'dissonance' can encourage many people to re-inspect, challenge and change some of their prejudgements. *Pretending that they don't exist is not going to help*. Mind you, there will be certain people who will recognise that they are prejudiced and simultaneously have no desire to change. Such prejudices are usually deeply and hotly held and are serving some emotional purpose – here, more than a purely rational intervention may be necessary before change is achieved.

So, the halo effect describes the way that people who have characteristics (from the left column) will tend to be seen in a very positive light. The halo effect influences how you see people and the work they do. For example, male students who read an essay by a girl they believe to be attractive rate the essay as better than if they believe the girl is unattractive.[8] As Aristotle said, 'Beauty is a greater recommendation than any letter of introduction.'

If children misbehave we judge them differently, according to their looks. The misbehaviour of the attractive child is explained away:

> She appears to be a perfectly charming little girl, well-mannered, basically unselfish. It seems that she can adapt well among children her age and make a good impression . . . she plays well with everyone, but like anyone else a bad day can occur. Her cruelty . . . need not be taken seriously.

The ugly child who has done exactly the same thing is seen as maladjusted and deviant:

> I think the child would be quite bratty and would be a problem to teachers . . . she would probably try to pick a fight with other children her own age . . . she would be a brat at home . . . all in all, she would be a real problem.[9]

Whereas we tend to be very concerned about racism and sexism, perhaps it's time to consider the area of 'looksism' – and 'heightism' as well. It's all too easy to get caught up with the latest fashion in what is considered to be a prejudice.

The 'horns effect' describes the way that a negative characteristic will adversely affect our whole judgement. If someone has characteristics (from the right column) we will tend to see him or her in a negative light.

Halo and horns are easily triggered. For example, take the old idea of 'What's in a name?' Take ten top academic journals. Select one article from each, published in the last two years, change the name of the author and institution to which he/she belongs, slightly reword the opening and resubmit it to the journal which published it. Describe the author as affiliated to the 'Bognor Regis' Polytechnic or 'the Northern Plains Centre for Human Understanding', instead of as coming from prestigious institutions like Harvard or Oxford. Such research[10] reveals that seven out of the ten articles resubmitted in this way go completely unrecognised and less than 20 per cent of the editors and reviewers recommended the articles for publication. The very journals that had previously published the almost identical articles now make comments about poor writing quality and weakness of methodology!

Forewarned Is?

How does what we hear or know about another affect how we see him or her? There is a classic experiment where two groups, A and B, were told that they were to be given a lecture by someone they did not know and whom they would subsequently be asked to judge. Both groups were given a description of him. Group A read that: 'Mr X is a graduate student in the Department of Economics and Social Science . . . He is 26 years old . . . and married. People who know him consider him to be a rather *warm* person [my emphasis], industrious, critical, practical and determined.'[11]

Group B received exactly the same description in every way except that the word *warm* was changed to *cold*.

Mr X then gave a talk to the two groups together. The students subsequently rated him:

> Although all of the students had been exposed to the same person at the same time, those who had been told that he was reputed to be 'warm' rated him as substantially more considerate, informal, sociable, popular, good-natured, humorous and humane than those who had been forewarned that he was 'cold'.[12]

Just the change of that one word – warm to cold – created this huge difference.

And you notice that the resulting effect of prior warning is not just to spot the mentioned characteristic. A specified characteristic can trigger perception of a whole set of other characteristics that are expected to accompany it. We then see the person in question in the light not just of the mentioned characteristic, but in terms of an entire expected 'type' of personality.

So, as usual, our mind-sets gear us to see what we expect to see. As part of a radio series I devised for the BBC, six people were invited to interview a solicitor and a BBC radio producer. Even though the six laughed much more during their four-minute interview with the solicitor than with the producer, it was the producer who was seen to be funnier. One wonders just how funny the solicitor would have needed to be before he was allowed to escape from the 'solicitor' category and all that goes with it.

The group also jumped to various conclusions about the solicitor which were often unfounded. Whereas the solicitor had said that he had attended a Catholic school, which to his surprise, he said, had recently become a public school, one of the interviewers told me just minutes afterwards that it was obvious that he would have gone to some sort of a public school. The same interviewer went on to say 'Although he didn't say, his children presumably are at private or public school – it's to be expected. But a likeable fellow.' His children are not at private or public school and I wonder what he meant by 'But a likeable fellow'![13]

Any 'label' will make us hypersensitive to any supporting evidence. The following research story illustrates the point well.[14] A group of eight men and women was formed to test the stickiness of psychiatric labels. The group members had different backgrounds – a housewife, a psychiatrist, three psychologists, a painter and so on. They contacted different psychiatric hospitals and complained of hearing a voice which seemed to say 'empty', 'hollow', 'thud'. All were admitted. As from the moment of admission they all stopped feigning these symptoms, voices, etc., and started to behave as 'normally' as they knew how. All were diagnosed as schizophrenic, except one who was diagnosed as 'a manic-depressive psychotic'. Each patient knew that discharge was dependent on proof of 'sanity'. Despite total remission of symptoms the pseudo-patients were kept in on average for nineteen days. The longest period was fifty-two days! Between them they were administered nearly 2,100 assorted pills (mostly flushed down the lavatory). During their enforced stay they kept notes of life on the inside. This, in itself was seen by some staff as proof of illness: 'Patient engages in writing behaviour.'

Another psychiatric hospital which had not been involved with any of these pseudo-patients boasted that such patients would not go unnoticed by them. It was agreed, therefore, to send to that hospital a number of pseudo-patients within a three-month period. The hospital judged that of the 193 patients admitted, 41 were pseudo-patients. In fact none had been sent!

There is an additional reason why it can be difficult for a group of people to get rid of a bad reputation. As previously mentioned, one reason for stereotypes and pigeon-holes is that we want to try and predict how we think another person will behave. Therefore in meeting people and evaluating their behaviour we tend to attribute that behaviour to the way we think *they actually are*, their disposition, rather than to the situation in which they find themselves. This can be a problem for any minority or disadvantaged group as the general public may decide that their misfortunes are a result of the way they are, as opposed to the circumstances which are hindering their progress and change.

So give a dog a bad name, or get off on the wrong foot and get yourself a label and you may have the utmost difficulty disposing of it. One implication for performance appraisal is the reading of personnel reports and the like, *after* the interview. Although this may be difficult in some cases, the principle can, none the less, often be applied.

First Impressions

Often we have no forward information when we meet people for the first time. There may be few expectations.

Imagine several observers who are asked to watch a student solve a series of problems at different times. There are 30 problems and unknown to the observers, by pre-arrangement, the student always scores 15 out of 30. Sometimes, however, the student bunches the correct answers towards the start of the 30, and at other times, towards the end. First of all those observers who see the student get the 15 right at the start of the 30 rate the subject as more intelligent, than other observers who see him get 15 out of 30 towards the end. Secondly, when recalling how many problems were correctly solved, observers who see front-end success say some 20.6, whereas those who see the success towards the end, say 12.5.[15] So, we 'lock into' these first impressions. A new grid is quickly formed and subsequent evidence is often forced to fit that grid.

The Judgement Grid

If you turn back to your Judgement Grid at the back of the book, you can now begin to identify another factor that biases your judgement of others. You have probably already marked certain characteristics as positive, neutral or negative. If you haven't added the weightings, you can now. As mentioned before, we are looking here at your psycho-logical world, so that you do not have to follow rules of logic – both characteristics in a pair could be positive or negative for you. You can simply code each characteristic as either + or − or 0 if it's neutral.

You can now see who you will tend to regard in a more positive or a more negative light. Those people you perceive as having characteristics which you rate as positive will tend to get more chances of a halo, and those with characteristics you have rated as negative, more of the horns. In other words, your own deep judgement grid is constantly influencing your judgement of others. This may be fine for working out who you want as your friends, but is it any basis for working out how to get through to another person or whether or not you should employ him or her?

Dancing the Dance

The 'self-fulfilling prophecy' describes the way that things have a habit of turning out in the way we expect them to. For example, in the context of meeting people, if you assume that the person you have just met is aggressive, you may behave aggressively towards him or her and so in turn he or she may respond aggressively. Our mind-set creates its own 'reality'.

> The candidates from prestigious schools . . . did not appear to be questioned as closely about the details of their research . . . We seemed to encourage such candidates to talk about the more interesting theoretical issues and, consequently, they themselves gave the impression of being more interesting and promising. Other candidates, for whom one or more of us had less favourable expectations, would get flooded with questions about abstruse statistical issues – to see if they knew what they were talking about – and their presentations would become bogged down in uninteresting detail. Hence, even if they did know their material perfectly, they appeared overly concerned with minutiae and much less interesting and/or promising.[16]

This sad trick of getting others to dance the dance you expect them to dance is not just brought about through the conversation we encourage. For example, one study showed that white interviewers are more successful in bringing out better white interviewee performance than white interviewers interviewing black interviewees – and this is where the interviewees have been selected for being very alike – only their colour was different. This came about through the white interviewers showing less 'immediacy' with the blacks than the whites – i.e. there was a greater distance between the two, less eye contact, less facing of the interviewee and leaning forward – and the interviewer was less comfortable as revealed by a higher rate of speech errors and the shorter time spent in the interview. Not surprisingly the black interviewees were more nervous and performed less well. In their turn they perceived the white interviewers as being less adequate and friendly than did the white interviewees.[17]

The Day of Judgement

Every day is a day of judgement – we judge others and they judge us. Good judges of character are aware of the range of factors that distort their impressions. And put at its simplest, good judges of character first of all realise that their beliefs about people are simply *tentative* ideas. They are not, and can never be, gospel.

Try to do the opposite of what you and most people normally do. That is, you usually try to confirm your opinions and beliefs about others. Instead try to *disprove* your opinion. In doing this you will develop a new and unique impression of each individual – which is surely what he or she deserves.

And remember – whenever people act in ways that fit your beliefs about them, they may only be playing out a role that you and others have given them and are expecting them to play now!

References

1. Sherwood, J.J. & Nataupsky, M. 'Predicting the conclusions of negro-white intelligence research from biographical characteristics of the investigator.' *Journal of Personality and Social Psychology*, 1968, Vol. 8, No. 1, pp. 53–58.
2. Sherwood, J.J. & Nataupsky, M. Ibid. p.57.
3. Oskamp, S. *Attitudes and Opinions*, Prentice-Hall, 1977, p.346.
4. Oskamp, S. Ibid. p.347.
5. Oskamp, S. Ibid. p.347.
6. Oskamp, S. Ibid. p.349.
7. The images shown here form part of a larger management development package entitled, 'Only Bigots Say They Have No Prejudices', information available from:

Customer Information Manager
Innovation Centre Europe Ltd
BCM Box 6
London WC1N 3XX
England
Tel: 0491 411173

8. Landy, D. & Sigall, H. 'Beauty is talent: Task evaluation as a function of the performer's physical attractiveness.' *Journal of Personality and Social Psychology*, 1974, 29, pp. 299–304.

9. Dion, K. K. 'Physical attractiveness and valuations of children's transgressions.' *Journal of Personality and Social Psychology*, 1972, 24, pp. 207–13.

10. Peters, D. & Ceci, S. 'A manuscript masquerade: how well does the review process work?' *The Sciences*, September 1980, Vol. 20, Part 7, pp. 16–21.

11. Kelley, H. H. 'The warm-cold variable in first impressions of persons.' *Journal of Personality*, 1950, 18, pp. 431–439.

12. Patton, B. R. & Giffin, K. *Interpersonal Communication in Action*, Harper & Row, 1977, p.151.

13. From 'Getting to Know You' – one of a series of pieces from 'In the Mind's Eye', devised and presented by myself for Radio 4's *Woman's Hour*, Spring, 1981. All thanks to producer Janet Thomas for her professional perseverance in translating the ideas into good radio.

14. Rosenhan, D. L. 'On being sane in insane places.' *Science*, Vol. 179, January 19, 1973, pp.250–258.

15. Jones, E. E., Rock, L., Shaver, K. G., Goethals, G. R. & Ward, L. M. 'Pattern of performance and ability attribution: An unexpected primacy effect.' *Journal of Personality and Social Psychology*, 1968, 9, pp. 317–340.

16. Jones, R. A. *Self-Fulfilling Prophecies*, Lawrence Erlbaum Associates, 1977, p.2.

17. Word, C. O., Zanna, M. P. & Cooper, J. 'The nonverbal mediation of self-fulfilling prophecies in interracial interaction.' *Journal of Experimental Social Psychology*, 1974, 10, pp. 109–120.

CHAPTER FIVE

'I Just Work Here'

There are two possible causes of psychological retirement. The first is where the individual and job are mismatched. The second is when the individual's and organisation's values (or function's) diverge.

Hurt or Ert?

The more an organisation talks about and runs seminars on motivation, the more you can guess you're involved in an old-world establishment. One of the most commonly asked questions of many a consultant is 'What can we do to motivate people?' And although I exaggerate to make the point, let's take the starting answer as *'Nothing'*. And in a strict sense the answer is correct. *There is nothing you can do directly to motivate another.*

In the same way that you can't 'laugh' or 'learn' people, you can't 'motivate' them. It makes equally bad sense (and is bad grammar) to ask the question in the first place. In the same way that it rains and it snows, people *are motivated*. The problem, however, is that they may not be motivated to do the things you wish them to! Gone are the days when we saw the sign 'Hands Wanted' on the side of the factory wall. The sign was very honest in its statement. 'Hands' were wanted – not the inconvenience of hearts, souls, bladders and personalities. You find there are increasingly few people who are happy for you to employ simply their hands – the whole person wants to come to work!

The question of 'how to motivate' seems to assume that people tend to be 'inert', passive or inactive. This manifestly is not the case. For example, if you were to put down this book, what would you do instead? You might sit and think, pick up a newspaper, write a letter, make a phone-call or go for a walk. *You would do something.* You are never completely inert, not even when day-dreaming or asleep. Human beings, as long as they are alive, are never inert. *They are active.* Or as psychologist, Guy Claxton, points out:

'They are ert.'[1]

They *ert* all over the place, in numerous different ways! And sure enough when we complain of a motivation problem we usually mean that people are not *erting* in the direction that we wish them to.

If you try to push them in a direction that is counter to their *ert* – it hurts. And true, if you hurt them enough, people will move and do things, at least for a short time. You can beat, threaten and bribe and get short-term movement from the other person, but you won't affect their longer-term motivation except, perhaps, for the worse. Therefore *ert* or hurt: the choice is simple and commonsensical.

Matching Ert and Job

The easiest way to tap someone's *ert* is to ask the person to do something they already want to do. Obviously enough, you select those people who enjoy doing the job in question – that is the actual range of activities that go to make up the job itself. In this way work is fun and productive. Yet, sadly for many the idea of work and 'a job' conjure up associations of boredom and drudgery. True enough, there may still be some jobs where it is hard to find anyone whose 'ert', or what makes them tick, can be matched to that job. But technology is doing away with more and more of these inhuman jobs.

The sceptic may still say that I am being too idealistic – 'Surely all jobs have a degree of routine in them? We can't "play" all the time? There are deadlines to be met and hard graft to be put in.' I agree. It may be difficult to have a constant 100 per cent total match to the job itself all of the time – that is, to the various activities within any job. This is where the *way in which you manage* and are managed can minimise any dissatisfaction brought on by any degree of 'activity' mismatch – that is, a mismatch between what makes you tick and the activities that constitute the job itself. We will have a look at setting this 'right climate' a little later. First of all let's concentrate on the most direct way of unleashing your own ert – doing what you want and being paid for it.

I recall a computer programmer who was literally in love with his job. It was his passion. 'Monday morning blues' were unknown to him. A spring in his foot and a gleam in his eye, he arrived at work passionately enthusiastic. His 'tick' or 'ert' (see Figure 5.1) were completely matched to his job. And, not surprisingly, he was very good at his job. To cap it all he seemed to have relentless energy. The more in tune you are with your ert, the more energy you have.

This computer programmer is an example of a perfect match. Relevant job skills were also present. You may come across such 'Happy Performers' in music, arts, sport – and even in business! I mention the world of music and arts because here you often meet people who have a passion and follow it through, perhaps regardless of short-term

Figure 5.1   The Happy Performer

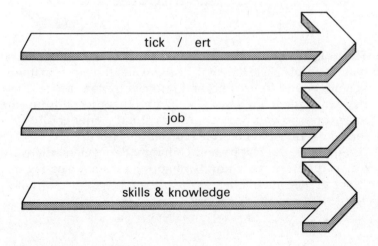

financial well-being. However, as we will see later, many of these people go on to enjoy a secure enough future, even if the path taken might appear somewhat precarious to other more conventional folk.

If the 'Happy Performers' (see Figure 5.1) have a complete match whereby all three lines run in parallel and so score 10, the 'Unhappy Performers' find that their tick and job lines are moving in opposite directions (see Figure 5.2). As they are unhappy 'performers', however, the skills line is running in parallel with the job line. The example in Figure 5.2 scores 0.

Figure 5.2   The Unhappy Performer

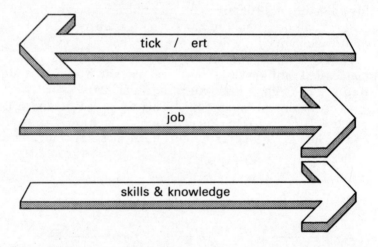

They can do their jobs. They have the skills. But they also hate their jobs. The less matched you are, the more apathetic you are bound to become, and if forced by conscience – 'fair pay for a good day's work' – or by others to perform, the more stressed you become. And, naturally enough, there is the whole range of possible scores from 0 to 10.

Alongside the Happy and Unhappy Performers, there are the 'Happy Learners' and 'Unhappy Learners' (see Figures

5.3 and 5.4), again with a continuum of scores from 0 to 10. In both these cases you need to develop or take on new skills and knowledge. The learning matches the job. As before, whether or not that job and its required learning make you happy or not is a matter of the ert or tick match.

Figure 5.3   The Happy Learner

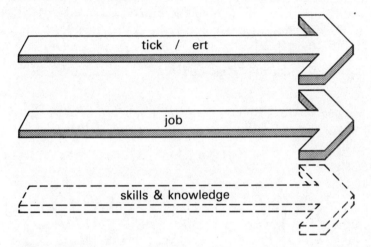

Figure 5.4   The Unhappy Learner

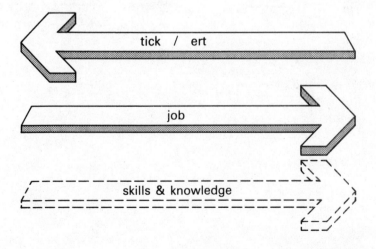

Using Figure 5.5, you can score yourself by way of (a) job match, and by way of (b) – your knowledge/skill level match for your present job.

So, there is just one desperate strategy you can use to motivate people directly – brain transplants – that is, give them someone else's ert that matches what you want. Otherwise, everything else that we can do to tap another's ert, comes down to helping the individual to ert or to 'tick' in the direction he or she wishes.

Figure 5.5   Job/Knowledge Match

(a) job match your ert/tick match with job itself

(b)   knowledge/skill level match

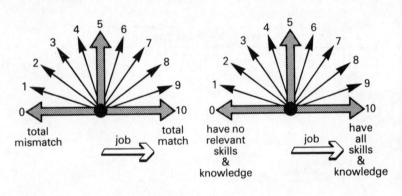

SCORE

SCORE

Matching Ert and Managing Ert

There is a plethora of management theories on motivation. Most managers have heard of Maslow's 'Hierarchy of
Needs'[2] and McGregor's 'Theory X and Y'.[3] To an extent,
what I have said so far about motivation is much influenced
by these and other writers, such as Frederick Herzberg.

It is not surprising that Herzberg's classic paper 'One more
time: How do you motivate employees?' originally published
in the *Harvard Business Review* in 1968, has sold more than 1.2
million reprints since publication.[4] This is the single largest
sale of any of the thousands of articles that the *Harvard
Business Review* have published. It is, indeed, an excellent
article. (Additional comments at the end of the 1987 reprint
are also helpful.[5])

Herzberg is important for several reasons. First of all
he distinguishes between those things that a manager can
do that create movement (i.e. threat and various forms of
'KITA' – or a 'kick in the ass') and those factors that release
another's intrinsic motivation or ert. The KITA factors he
calls 'hygiene factors' and the growth or ert factors he names
'motivators'. The hygiene factors, which are 'extrinsic' to
the job itself, and to do with conditions of work, include
your company policy, procedures, supervision and salaries,
relationships with other people at work, physical working
conditions and job security.

The 'motivators' are intrinsic to the job itself. This therefore includes the job match, in terms of whether you are
a happy or unhappy performer or learner. Then there are
additional factors—and *these are factors that can be managed from
day to day*. It is here that there is scope for setting, indirectly
that is, an 'erting' environment. These additional intrinsic
factors include, for example, recognition, responsibility,
achievement and possibility for growth and advancement.

Secondly, Herzberg points out that although lack of hygiene factors will create dissatisfaction, their fulfilment in
abundance will not necessarily motivate. In other words,
you need to look after these 'lower' needs so as to get to
base camp. If you then want to climb the mountain, you
start to focus on the 'higher' motivators.

Matching and Shedding

What does this mean in practice? We must always look after working conditions adequately, otherwise we run the risk of turning people off. And we want to ensure that we have a good job match. The question is simple: 'Will you or do you enjoy the actual activity of the job itself?' If not, don't take the job, or do a different one. If you are already in the job, consider what can be done to increase those parts that you enjoy and reduce those you don't. In fact, this will always be a problem. As you become competent in the different parts of your job you may no longer find certain activities continue to be intrinsically motivating. There is, therefore, a need to shed those parts. Successful job design allows an individual to pass over these parts to another person who, in his or her turn, finds those activities rewarding. Some form of 'job enrichment' is, therefore, essential if you wish to retain your own and others' ert.

Job enrichment does not simply mean expanding a job. It means building on what:

the other likes doing,
and the way they like to be managed –

in other words the higher motivators of achievement and recognition and the like. The intrinsic motivating factors always fall into these two camps – the job itself and the way that we manage the individual.

When it comes to managing the individual, there is a central difficulty: How do you work out what another person's higher motivators are – that is how it is they like to be managed, have goals set, rewarded and the like? Some people are turned on by power, others by achievement, responsibility, recognition, growth and opportunity for learning and challenge and so on. In fact, many of us are turned on by a range of these in differing amounts. And some of these factors may turn some of us off. The questionnaire at the end of this chapter enables you to think through the relevant importance of a range of extrinsic and intrinsic factors.

So we are back to the old problem. Most management theories, be they to do with motivation, leadership or selling, are what I've called 'grand' in their design. They tell us about people and the world at large. On the other hand all individuals are unique. And although it makes for supposedly bad English, it is true to say that all of us are *very* or *extraordinarily unique*. In which case what can these very general theories tell us about any one unique individual? Probably not too much. Yet, if I push my argument that people are very different to the extreme, these theories are of no use at all. And the busy manager may feel that he or she just doesn't have the time to climb into every other person's world to find out what makes them tick in his or her unique way. Ert or no ert, there is still a job to be done! Can't these theories be used as a guideline at least?

There seem to be a couple of ways round this problem. The first is that you don't need to create a unique and total working theory as to how every other person ticks. It comes down to getting into the other's world and trying to get *some idea* of how he or she feels and thinks about things. This gives you a tentative idea of what makes them tick. You proceed, again tentatively, and if your approach isn't working you modify your idea or 'model' of the other and try again.

Secondly, the various theories that exist, again be they about motivation, leadership, selling or whatever, can at least provide a useful starting-point for trying to figure out the other person's world. And this is the key – any theory is used only as a tentative base-camp.

Type 1 and Type 2 Use of Theories

'There is nothing more practical than a good theory.'[6] This is, at least, sometimes true. It depends if the theory is applied in a Type 1 or Type 2 manner. If a Type 1 manager takes a theory on board, he or she will usually become stuck with it. The theory becomes the *truth*. And all people are then subsumed, understood and treated in terms of the theory.

A Type 2 approach recognises the value of the theory as a stepping-stone that may guide and offer some insight, but will never be absolutely true in any one case. And whereas a Type 1 manager will be attracted to rather simplistic models that reduce uncertainty and ambiguity, Type 2's may well prefer more sophisticated and potentially more helpful models. In this respect it is interesting to note the sales success of some very popular management books that push highly simplified, some might say trite, theories of us very complex human beings – some of which, for example, assume that there are, say, three secret rules to successful people management. If only it were so simple!

It clearly isn't simple. And some theories begin to acknowledge the complexity of *Homo sapiens*. Alongside the approaches to motivation mentioned so far, there is another, called 'Values Analysis', which is based on the surprisingly under-acknowledged work of American psychologist, Clare Graves.[7] He produced a seven-level model of human development. The usefulness of the model is again that it gives you a possible insight into other people's worlds. The model is also interesting in that it can be seen to contradict some of the other models that, perhaps over-simply, suggest that once the lower 'hygiene' factors have been cared for, attention can then productively be focused on the higher motivators. Perhaps, some people, although we would hope a small minority, are not receptive, at present, to such higher factors.

The seven stages reflect different types of concerns and values. Graves suggests that as we mature we progress from one level or value system to another. Whereas, he maintains, most reach stages 4 or 5, few reach stage 7:

> . . . employees with tribalistic values [level 2] re-
> spond best to a benevolently autocratic management
> style . . . while egocentrics [level 3] would view
> such an approach as so weak and indecisive as to
> invite disobedience. Absolutist [level 4] employees,
> on the other hand, expect to be treated in a dignified,
> business-like manner and take comfort in clear-cut
> rules and procedures. Achievists [level 5] will chafe
> under those same rules; they value the end, not
> the means, and respond to material rewards for
> achieving goals. Such incentives, however, would

mean little to a sociocentric [level 6] person, who would much rather have a harmonious and mutually supportive relationship with his co-workers. Finally, the individualist [level 7] takes pride in achievement – not so much for reward but for the feeling of being part of a dynamic and successful enterprise.[8]

This and other models do not give us the truth but they can help fire the imagination. They enable us to understand how others may tick and therefore what we need to do to manage more effectively. The model, however, is always a starting-point. As soon as you find that you are instantly stereotyping another within a label provided by the model you can be fairly sure that you are missing out on the uniqueness of the other.

Values Match

Not only do we want a motivational match, we also want a 'values' match. Here, we are talking about matching the 'personality' of the organisation and the people working within that organisation.

To appreciate more fully the nature of values, some examples may be of help. Apple Computer's values were noted in Chapter 1. Hewlett Packard present theirs as:

- Trust,
- Openness,
- Informality,
- Managing by walking around,
- Sharing,
- MBO (management by objectives),
- Enthusiasm,
- 'Small is beautiful'.[9]

Like Apple's, these sound really positive. However, in many companies, the truth is often far from being so simple. A couple of years ago I worked with two service organisations – one huge public sector organisation employing some 200,000 people, and the other a smaller private sector company. In both cases I was involved from the top down, in teasing out the present values of the organisations and then establishing what the values needed to be so as 'to ensure the continuing and growing success' of the two organisations.

Amongst the 'present values' the following less positive or negative values emerged:

> Us and them,
> Low personal reward,
> Cynicism,
> Compromise management,
> Standing/status,
> Resistance to the new,
> Customers – an inconvenience.

So, clearly an organisation can hold negative values. Furthermore many of the positive values may only receive lip-service support.

A company may also hold contradictory values. This is well-illustrated in the area of customer care.

Taking the idea that the customer is both internal and

Figure 5.6   Positive Flow

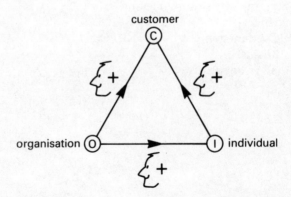

external, ideally the organisation – that is the people generally—care about the internal individuals *and* care about the
external customer. In this way the triangle flows positively,
as in Figure 5.6. Here there would be a general value of
customer care, internal and external.

Figure 5.7 Lack of Internal Care

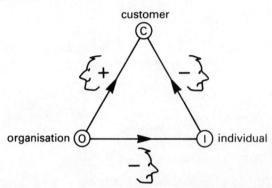

However, you may find that the value of external customer
care is espoused by the organisation, but that there is little
or no internal care for your own people/customers (see
Figure 5.7). Not surprisingly it may be difficult for your own
people then to provide care for the external customer.[10] It is
possible to achieve the situation shown in Figure 5.8, but this
depends upon having individuals who have a pride in their
job, despite the low caring attitude of the organisation. Your
people are much more likely to care about your customers,
if you, as an organisation care fully about them.

*Figure 5.8 Low Internal Care but High Care for External
Customer*

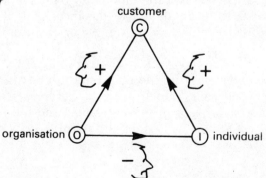

Sadly there are many organisations who care not much for their own, nor the customer, as in Figure 5.9. There is finally, at least theoretically, the case of the organisation whose profile looks like that shown in Figure 5.10.

Figure 5.9   Low Care All Round

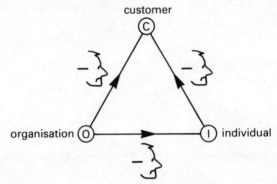

Figure 5.10   The Organisation That Looks After its Own

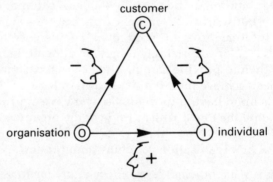

Here the organisation cares about its own but does not expect any care to be shown to the inconvenient punter. Perhaps this describes a POW camp – or even some public sector organisations!

These 'present values' affect the workings of the organisation today. When thinking about the future you want to consider what your values need to become. There will either be no gap between present values and future values (I haven't yet found such an organisation), a small or larger gap. Clearly it is very important to generate these future values in such a way that all members of your organisation feel they own them.

For example, for the smaller private sector company, in which I was working on this question of values, we generated the following list and explanation of future values. Using the theme of 'Creating Our Future', these values were agreed as follows (the list does not suggest level of importance – they are all equally important):

> *Customer care* – there is perhaps nothing more important than turning to face the customer – listening and really understanding their point of view and providing what they want in the way that they want.
> *Consistent and ever-increasing quality* – not only do we want to be known as an organisation that already provides consistent quality – we want our customers to see that this quality is improving over time.
> *Initiative (accountability and responsibility)* – this is the very simple value stressing the importance of once you have had a good idea – do something!
> *People first* – we recognise there is nothing more important than our customers and our own people – these two factors together making us successful. This naturally includes treating people honestly and fairly.
> *Fun and enjoyment* – this is the idea that work should not be drudgery – that people should derive constant satisfaction from the work they do.
> *Commitment and involvement (I/we are the organisation/company)* – this value recognises the need to have everyone as part of the organisation, being well-informed and so identifying directly with the organisation.
> *Profit* – many people would say that this is the key value – without this we cannot achieve any of the others. (Some say that 'profit' is not so much a 'value', at least that is within commercial organisations. It may be that here profit is an objective rather than a value.)
> *Teamwork* – here we have the value that highlights the importance of working together in such a way

that the whole is more than the sum of the parts.

Encouraging the new – this is the belief in the importance of coming up with relevant new products/
services/ways of doing things and also finding new
ways of providing existing products and services.
Clearly if we do not come up with new ideas, we
will lose competitive edge – coming up with the new
ideas and turning them into action is key.

Recognition and reward – here we stress the importance
of rewarding and recognising each other in the way
that we treat, speak with and pay ourselves.

One clearly contrasting value between the small private
sector company and the huge public sector one was the
respective use of the words 'people/us' and 'staff/them'.

Your Organisation's and Function's Values

Jot down what you feel are your organisation's values. If you
feel that your function's or department's values are different
from the organisation's, create a separate list.

Present values

Organisation   Function

_____   _____

_____   _____

_____   _____

_____   _____

_____   _____

_____   _____

_____   _____

_____   _____

_____   _____

(You may also wish to code any that you feel are stated but that only receive lip-service support. You may also spot certain contradictory values.)

The following list of mainly positives, with a few negatives, may act as a prompt or a reminder of your organisation's/function's values:

Highest quality/value
Excellence
Innovation
Initiative
Profitability
Customer/client service
No personal reward
Lack of involvement
Caring for our own people
Clear and shared vision
Highest levels of
  performance
Commitment
Paternalism
Effectiveness
Productivity
Friendly
Fun
Inspirational
Motivational
Stimulation
Competitiveness

Delegation to lowest
  possible level
Responsibility
Accountability
Status-conscious
Self-interest
'I just work here'
Integrity
Trust
Teamwork
Good communications/
  well-informed people
Carelessness
Us and them
Open
Formal
Enthusiasm
Political
Suspicious
Challenge
Positive social contribution

What values do you believe your organisation needs so as to ensure its growing and continuing success? Here, you notice there will be no gap between the organisation and the function. Such a division is only indicative of an old-world and segmentalist organisation – and I doubt if that is any formula for future success.

Future values

_____

_____

_____

_____

_____

_____

_____

_____

The sceptic at this point, I feel, may say, it's all very well going through these top-level cerebral fitness exercises, but what real difference does it make at the cutting face of the organisation? Does the customer ever see a difference? Does it have any positive impact on the bottom line?

Well, if the exercise stops at senior level and is not passed down the organisation so that new patterns of behaviour emerge which are congruent with the new values, clearly the whole exercise is a waste of time. More than that, it may be counter-productive, as some people may have higher expectations and then even lower ones than they originally had when they find the status quo remains.

Changing Your Organisation's Values

There are two approaches I have used to get round this problem. To ensure that the values are passed right down throughout the organisation we have either done a full:

'7 S Analysis'

or set up appropriate

'Leading Edge Teams'

or both.

Figure 5.11   The 7–S Framework[11]

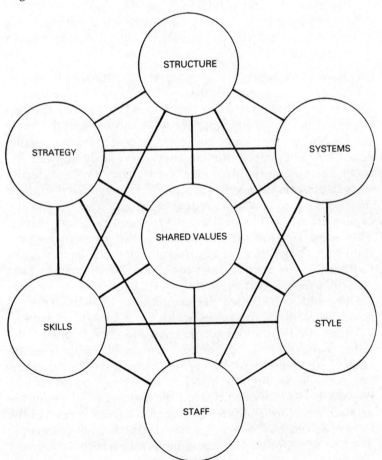

The '7 S' model is simple, fairly well-known and easy to understand.

The model highlights several dimensions that need to be considered in thinking about any organisation. There is the:

> 1. Strategy – that is, where you are aiming to get to.
> 2. Structure describes the shape of your organisation – flat, hierarchical, etc.
> 3. Systems include distribution and information methods.
> 4. Staff considers the people you have and need, don't need or don't, at this point, have.
> 5. Skills follow on and focus on who needs to be able to do and know what.
> 6. Style looks at the way in which you do things – are you paternalistic, participative, authoritarian, etc., in your style?

Lastly, underpinning these outer six S's, there is a central S (shared) – or, in my experience, just plain V – for Values. Ideally you find that there are 'Shared Values' within an organisation that are compatible with and support the outer six S's. Sadly the truth is that the values of many an organisation are not shared, nor do they necessarily support the outer S's. Among senior management there may be differing views about its values. Further down the organisation there may be very low awareness of what the top espouses as the organisation's values or there may be contradictory values. This is perhaps most clearly seen in some companies where there is a large management/union or work-force divide. Furthermore in many British companies, there may be little open discussion had or encouraged about what the values are or need to be. Open discussion about values may well be an indicator of corporate health.

There is clearly a danger in trying to change one of the outer S's if that change is not compatible with the core values, be these held by 'senior' folk only or generally. For example, in one organisation, an attempt to restructure the organisation was hampered by the re-emergence of the original structure and lines of communication, almost in the form of an old-boy network. The old structure is what people liked, understood and valued. The question is therefore how to set about changing these core values and ensuring that they are fairly universally shared. You can then begin to change some of the outer 'S's' more easily and effectively.

In the first place, the Board (and perhaps certain top teams) need to analyse their existing values and generate future ones that will ensure, they feel, their success. Then the top teams generate goals, be these problems or opportunities, that need to be addressed in the light of shifting from the existing to the future values. Each goal or issue is identified under one of the outer six S's. For example, one top team might decide that in the light of the required future value of 'flexibility' there is a goal/problem: 'To eliminate risk aversion throughout the business', and that this goal falls under the heading of 'style'. In the light of the required future value of accountability the goal is: 'To establish clear accountabilities and reward systems', and this goal falls under the heading of 'systems' and 'style'.

These goals are then tackled, using a process of creative problem-solving, as described in Chapters 8 and 9, or are passed on down the organisation to functions/teams that are most appropriately involved in thinking through and owning the issue. Not surprisingly, this 'passing on' of predetermined goals, may, in some cases meet with resistance if people do not understand and appreciate the new values which have given rise to the goals. Assuming the new values have been explained, asking teams to address practical goals designed to achieve those values can be a very powerful and effective way to help people internalise and act on the new values.

'Leading Edge Teams' is another mechanism for ensuring that your new and desired values are translated into action. (See Figure 5.12) Leading Edge Teams are teams who are skilled in creative problem solving (again described in Chapters 8 and 9). Rather than the top team or teams deciding on the goals which need to be addressed, the top team process stops one stage earlier. That is, they decide what are the required future values and then ask Leading Edge Teams throughout the organisation to generate goals, be they problems or opportunity areas, relevant to the achieving of any or all of those values. In this way the focus of the goal can be tied to the responsibilities and interest of the team concerned. This makes it most likely that the team will not

Figure 5.12   Changing Values

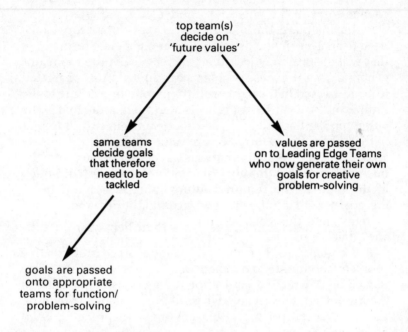

only be able to take the goal and generate ideas – but that they will also want and be able to implement many of the selected ideas themselves. Therefore their actions are congruent with the new values and relevant to their own activities. This process, along with Leading Edge Teams, is more fully discussed in Chapter 9.

Motivation Questionnaire

This questionnaire has been designed so that you can fill it in whilst reading this book – and yet also copy it to distribute to colleagues, those working for you, or if you run seminars, for seminar members. If you guess that you may want others to fill it in, obviously copy it, before filling it in yourself.

Enjoying Your Job?

And why shouldn't people have jobs they enjoy? If you stop and think about it, it makes a lot of sense.

If you enjoy your job, you have fun and you do the job more enthusiastically and effectively. Therefore it's in everybody's interest to make sure that you are in the best job possible.

That's what this questionnaire is about. You will get a good idea of what makes you 'tick' and how far your present job suits you.

And here is probably the most important point:
Do fill it in honestly.
You can't score badly!

The goal of these simple questions is to help you on the path of finding even more satisfaction and enjoyment in your daily work.

Thank you and have fun.

(And do feel free to change the wording of any of the questions so that they fit you more exactly.)

1.
Explanation:
Most jobs are made up of many parts. For example there are the actual everyday activities you do, through to the general environment in which you work. This question is solely about the activities that go to make up a job.
This question helps you find out how you feel about all those different activities.
A. How important is the actual work, that is the different activities that make up a job, for your motivation and satisfaction?

Please score:

Not at all   Totally

0   5   10

B. Please specify the different parts or activities within your present job (as few or many as you like) and then the percentage time (roughly) spent on those different parts – adding up to 100 per cent.

Finally can you please then indicate how far you enjoy doing those individual parts.

Please score:

Part/Activity	% No	Enjoyment	Total
1. _____	__ 0 _____	5 _____	10
2. _____	__ 0 _____	5 _____	10
3. _____	__ 0 _____	5 _____	10
4. _____	__ 0 _____	5 _____	10
5. _____	__ 0 _____	5 _____	10
6. _____	__ 0 _____	5 _____	10
7. _____	__ 0 _____	5 _____	10
8. _____	__ 0 _____	5 _____	10
9. _____	__ 0 _____	5 _____	10

(100 per cent total)

2.

Explanation:

Money – what a thorny topic! Assuming you are not starving to death (and how could you be in your organisation!), money is often seen to be one of those factors that's a problem if you don't have enough. But after a certain level of comfort it may become less motivating of itself.

See what you think:

A. How important for your motivation/satisfaction at work is the financial reward you receive for a job?

Not at all Totally

| 0 | 5 | 10 |

B. How satisfied are you with your present job's
financial reward?

Not at all Totally

| 0 | 5 | 10 |

3.
Explanation:
Some of us like being in a position of authority/power and
being able to exercise control over people and events.
How about you?
A. How important for your motivation/satisfaction at
work is the amount of power/authority/control you can
exercise?

Not at all Totally

| 0 | 5 | 10 |

B. How satisfied are you with
the amount of power/authority/control
in your present job?

Not at all Totally

| 0 | 5 | 10 |

4.
Explanation:
Some of us like to be able to see real achievement through
our work. For example, there are some jobs that are more a
question of maintaining or overseeing a process or system,
whereas others allow you to see the concrete results of your
individual effort.
What about you?
A. How important for your motivation/satisfaction at work
is the scope for achievement that a job provides?

Not at all   Totally

_____
0   5   10

B. How satisfied are you with your present job's
scope for achievement?

Not at all   Totally

_____
0   5   10

5.
Explanation:
Some people can go through life and not care too much
what other people think of them. Others like to receive some
acknowledgement and recognition.
What about you?
A. How important for your motivation/satisfaction at work
is the degree of acknowledgement/recognition you receive?

Not at all   Totally

_____
0   5   10

In that acknowledgement/recognition can come from different people/sources:

Customers/clients   _____
Superiors   _____
Peers   _____
Subordinates   _____
Direct pay   _____
Indirect benefits   _____   Please specify _____

. . .can you please show your *preference* (i.e acknowledgement from your peers may be much more important for you
than, say, extra pay), using:
5 – Most important
4 – Next most important
3 – Next most important
2 – Next most important
1 – Next most important
0 – Least important
And if some sources are equally important you can simply
tie two or more of them.

       . B. How satisfied are you with the degree
of acknowledgement you receive in your current job?

Not at all   Totally
_____
0   5   10

And please from where *most* acknowledgement comes from:

5 – Most
4 – Next most
3 – Next most
2 – Next most
1 – Next most
0 – Least or none
Or if you prefer use percentages (total 100 per cent)

Customers/clients   _____
Superiors   _____
Peers   _____

Subordinates   _____
Direct pay   _____
Indirect benefits   _____   Please specify _____

6.
Explanation:
Some of us are loners and others much more sociable.
Some of us are both.
What about you?
A. How important for your motivation/satisfaction at work
is friendship with colleagues?

Not at all   Totally
_____
0   5   10

B. How satisfied are you with the degree of friendship
with your current work colleagues?

Not at all   Totally
_____
0   5   10

7.
Explanation:
Some people are much affected by the place in which they
work.
What about you?
A. How important for your motivation/satisfaction at work
are the physical working conditions and surroundings?

Not at all   Totally
_____
0   5   10

B. How satisfied are you with your
current physical working conditions and surroundings?

Not at all   Totally

---

0   5   10

8.
Explanation:
We all have 'values' – principles that we believe in strongly.
Clearly different people have different values – a member of
the Mafia probably has very different values from a Christian
missionary or famine relief worker. Organisations also have
values that go to make up the culture of that organisation.

Does it matter to you if your values fit those values found
in your part of the organisation?
A. How important for your motivation/satisfaction at work
is it that your own values are the same as or similar to those
of the area/department/function you work in?

Not at all   Totally

---

0   5   10

B. And to what extent are your own values
the same as or similar to those of
your current area/department/function?

Not at all   Totally

---

0   5   10

9.
Explanation:
Well, you may say that your part of the organisation has different values to other parts of the organisation (if not, simply skip this question):
A. How important for your motivation/satisfaction at work is it that your own values are the same as or similar to those of the organisation (as you believe them to be)?

Not at all   Totally

0   5   10

B. To what extent are your own values the same as or similar to those of the organisation?

Not at all   Totally

0   5   10

10.
Explanation:
Going places – promotion and all that. Some people are keen to climb the promotions ladder, others happier where they are.
And you?
A. How important for your motivation/satisfaction at work is a good chance of relevant promotion?

Not at all   Totally

0   5   10

B. And to what extent do you feel your current job offers you a good chance of relevant promotion?

Not at all		Totally
0	5	10

11.
Explanation:
With the various home responsibilities people have, job security can be a key issue.
How about you?
A. How important for your motivation/satisfaction at work is job security?

Not at all		Totally
0	5	10

B. And to what extent do you feel your current job offers you job security?

Not at all		Totally
0	5	10

All people are unique. Therefore there are now some questions you are invited to fill in for aspects of working life that have not been mentioned so far but which are important for you – examples could include scope for:

Creativity/innovation
Developing new skills
Acquiring new knowledge
Self-fulfilment/self-esteem
Status and prestige
Setting own goals and standards

So, if you like, over to you:

12.
A. How important for your motivation/satisfaction at work
is

_____

_____

_____?

Not at all   Totally

0   5   10

B. And to what extent does your present job _____

_____

_____

_____?

Not at all   Totally

0   5   10

13.
A. How important for your motivation/satisfaction at work
is

_____

_____

_____?

Not at all	Totally	
0	5	10

B. And to what extent does your present job _____

_____

_____

_____?

Not at all		Totally
0	5	10

14.
A. How important for your motivation/satisfaction at work
is

_____

_____

_____?

Not at all		Totally
0	5	10

B. And to what extent does your present job _____

_____

_____

_____?

Not at all   Totally

---

0   5   10

16.
A. How important for your motivation/satisfaction at work
is

_____

_____

_____ ?

Not at all   Totally

---

0   5   10

B. And to what extent does your present job   _____

_____

_____

_____ ?

Not at all   Totally

---

0   5   10

What action now?

In the case of question 1, you can think through how to
shed responsibly those parts of your job you don't enjoy,

and consider what you can do to increase the percentage of those parts that you do enjoy.

For question 5, you can consider what can be done to ensure that you receive most/more acknowledgement/recognition from those sources which are most/more preferred by you.

For the remaining questions, look at the (A) scores that are roughly 7 or above, where the (B) score is below 7. What do you need to do to increase the (B) score? Have you discussed this with your manager, you human resource/personnel function, your work colleagues, friends, family, etc?

References

1. Claxton, G. *Live and Learn: An Introduction to the Psychology of Growth and Change in Everyday Life*, Harper & Row, 1984.
2. Maslow, A. H. *Motivation and Personality*, Harper & Row, 1954.
3. McGregor, D. *The Human Side of Enterprise*, McGraw-Hill, 1960.
4. Herzberg, F. 'One more time: How do you motivate employees?' *Harvard Business Review*, January-February 1968, pp. 53–62.
5. Herzberg, F. 'One more time: How do you motivate employees?' HBR Classic, *Harvard Business Review*, September-October 1987, pp. 109–120.
6. I don't know who said this – and I'd love to know.
7. See: Graves, C. W. 'The deterioration of work standards.' *Harvard Business Review*, September-October 1966, pp. 117–128.
   Graves, C. W. 'Levels of existence: an open system theory of values.' *Journal of Humanistic Psychology*, Volume X, No. 2, Fall 1970, pp. 131–155.
8. Howard, N. 'How good is values analysis?' in *Motivation of Personnel*, Timpe, A. D. (Ed.), Gower, 1986.
9. Bovin, O. Background paper on Hewlett Packard from Economist Conference Unit conference, 'Intrapreneurship in Practice', London, September 20, 1985.
10. Many thanks to Belinda Leslie for her insights into the way a public service may try to offer the value of 'care' to its external customers and yet show little or no care towards its own internal customers/people.
11. Pascale, T. R. & Athos, A. G. *The Art of Japanese Management*, Simon and Schuster, 1981. The same model is also associated with the management consultancy, McKinsey and Company, Inc.
    See Waterman Jr., R. H. *The Renewal Factor*, Bantam Press, 1988, pp. 57–70 for a development of the 7–S framework and the introduction of the 7–C framework.

CHAPTER SIX

The Success Profile

The Death of the 'Wally'

I recall being surprised, annoyed and disappointed when several managers working for one of the world's largest computer companies, kept referring to certain work colleagues as 'wallies'. I had expected a more enlightened and perhaps charitable point of view. The assumption being expressed, as I understood it, was that certain individuals were 'write-offs', in the sense of there being no chance of competence and development. There was the apparently shared sense that some people are just plain 'stupid' or 'dumb' and there is nothing you can do about it: 'You are as you are and no amount of thinking will change it.'

Shortly after and inspired by this experience I gave a paper at the Institute of Personnel Management National Conference, attacking the idea that anyone is or ever can be a 'wally' – thus the theme 'the death of the "wally"' – in the sense that no human being is plain stupid or dumb. We are all, in fact, the opposite – brilliant.[1]

> Nobody starts off stupid. You only have to watch babies and infants, and think seriously about what all of them learn and do, to see that, except for the most grossly retarded, they show a style of life, and a desire and ability to learn that in an older person we might well call genius.[2]

(There is increasing evidence that the supposedly 'grossly re-
tarded' also have huge potential, which has previously gone
unrecognised.) Organisations can therefore help nurture or
stifle this genius and brilliance.

Meanwhile, advocates of the idea that wallies do exist, may
also be fans of the Peter Principle. This is an idea some managers appear to delight in, which says that another manager
(not themselves!) who can do a job will get promoted. In turn
if he or she can do the next job, promotion will usually follow
– until such time that the individual is promoted to his or her
level of incompetence – that is the level at which they can
no longer cope. Some may even joke that such a person will
again be promoted to even giddier heights as no department
wants him around to mess things up!

A danger with this principle is that it obscures two greater
reasons why a manager performs less than optimally. These
two reasons also reveal that all of us can achieve much more
than we might otherwise think. The Peter Principle, on the
other hand, holds out little hope for improved performance.
The following two alternative reasons, however, show there
is room for tremendous and appropriately placed optimism.

The first of these two reasons has already been discussed
in detail within the question of motivation. The dedicated
doctor who dies of boredom when promoted to 'admin', for
instance, or the once highly motivated salesman, now sales
manager, who dreams longingly of past victories in the land
of selling. These casualties are not proof of any Peter Principle
– they reflect poor matching of the motivational bride and
the organisational groom. Again you are seeing round pegs
in square holes.

I Am as I Am and No Amount of Thinking
Will Change It

The second reason explains why most people perform below
par and why probably all of us perform below what is
possible. It is to do with the person's 'self-concept' – that is,
the type of person you believe yourself to be and potential you
believe you have. And right there in the phrase 'the potential

you believe you have', lies much of the problem. People usually only achieve the potential they *think* they have. It is their thinking that stops them achieving more – not their God-given – or genetic – potential.

What is being discussed here is not the power of 'positive thinking'. The mechanism by which a person only achieves what he or she believes possible is, as discussed in Chapter 4, the 'self-fulfilling prophecy'. This well-established notion suggests that you will behave towards others according to your beliefs about them *and that you will behave in your own life in a way which is consistent with your beliefs and self-concept*. In turn, this self-concept is influenced by how others see and treat you. In the same way we largely construct 'the world out there' we also *construct* our own sense of self.

The self-fulfilling prophecy (sometimes known as the Pygmalion effect) is witnessed in a range of situations. Imagine, for example, a perfectly creditworthy bank. Rumours are wrongly started to the effect that the bank is going broke. Understandably people start to remove their money, encouraging more people to do the same and so the bank goes broke. This spiral of belief or confidence which creates its own 'reality', for better or worse, is witnessed in the world of commodities through to the stock markets. The 'ultimate function of a prophecy is not to tell the future, but to make it'.[3]

Political and social behaviour can also take the form of the prophecy. 'While some serious and basic conflicts of interest may be unavoidable, warlike solutions spring always from warlike expectancies and preparation. The confirmed Marxist who sees class warfare (world-wide revolution preceded by imperialistic wars) as inevitable is merely *seeing* them as inevitable. If enough people on both sides of a dispute see the matter in the same way, then of course such wars *become* inevitable!'[4]

Likewise, if enough people in the world believe that famine is inevitable . . .

Prophecies can also affect how animals perform. For example, rats which are believed by experimenters to be 'bright' out-perform other rats believed to be 'dumb' in such tasks as finding their way through a maze.[5]

However, in our case, it is humans we are most interested

in. One early classic study of the prophecy at work went
as follows. A group of individuals were trained to produce
550 units of work (cards to be punched on a machine like
a typewriter) a day. They only exceeded this level of 550
units 'at great emotional cost'. The work-force was then
supplemented by individuals who knew nothing of the 550
limit. Soon, although members of 'the initial group were
exhausted after producing 700 cards per day, members of
the new group began turning out three times that number
without ill effects.'[6]

Another example of the prophecy at 'work' involved a
group of female employees who were given intelligence and
finger/dexterity tests. The foremen who were to supervise
the women were given the results, or at least that is what
they thought. They were actually fed false results. However,
where the result of the test was positive the foremen rated the
women more favourably than where the result of the tests
was negative. Furthermore the foremen's expectation also
affected the behaviour of the employees as '. . . the objective
production record of the workers was superior if the foremen
had expected superior performance.'[7]

Perhaps the most fascinating and well-known example
of the prophecy 'at school' is the famous Rosenthal and
Jacobson study.[8] In this case, at the end of one school year,
children were given an IQ test. Supposedly based on the
results of this test, teachers were told that a specific 20 per
cent of the children were expected to blossom intellectually.
In fact, the names making up that 20 per cent given to the
teachers were selected at random. When retested several
times over the next year, the scores showed that the greatest
gain came from that designated 20 per cent. And:

> . . . children from whom intellectual growth was
> expected were described as having a better chance of
> being successful in later life and being happier, more
> curious and more interesting than the other children.
> There was also a tendency for the designated children
> to be seen as more appealing, better adjusted and
> more affectionate, and less in need of social
> approval.[9]

Remember the 20 per cent had been, in fact, selected randomly!

More recently, it has been shown that the students' expectations of the teacher affects the teacher's and in turn the students' own success:

> Two classes of Canadian high schoolers, who had been given a glowing report on their new teacher, achieved significantly higher final grades in a three-week unit and participated more during class than students in classes who had been given no such expectations. The teacher was unaware that her abilities had been praised to the students.[10]

Various mechanisms have been suggested to explain how the prophecy is communicated. Contributory factors include: the amount of visual attention given to those learners from whom high performance is expected, expression of greater satisfaction, encouragement and praise, calling on the individuals, and communicating more with them in a more supporting, accepting and positive way.[11]

Now the sceptic might say, surely the prophecy will affect only those people who are impressionable – which largely means young children. Surely we robust adults will not be affected by what others think – it must just be kids' stuff.

What more robust world can you get than the army. In the context of a fifteen-week combat command course, instructors were given information about the trainees' 'command potential'. As you've guessed, the information, unknown to the instructors, was rigged: 'Trainees of whom instructors had been induced to expect better performance scored significantly higher on objective achievement tests, exhibited more positive attitudes, and perceived more positive leadership behavior.'[12]

'After the course we debriefed the instructors. The expectancy induction was so effective that it was difficult to convince the instructors that it had been random.'[13] In other words, when we have an expectation about another, it becomes so real that we cannot believe that it was not simply the other person. The prophecy applies, therefore to young

and adult alike. If only we all shared the justifiably positive
expectation about everyone's learning ability and potential –
just imagine what we could begin to achieve.

Where is all this potential?

Now, why do we allow ourselves to be limited by our
self-concept and the way others treat us? Perhaps, we seek
a high degree of consistency and certainty – so surpassing
our self-concept – and others' expectations – may rock
the psychological boat. Secondly, most older children and
adults work very hard at playing a game I call 'Statues'. To
play this bizarre and tragic game, you simply have to accept
the Type 1 banner: 'I am as I am and no amount of thinking
will change it.' In other words, you believe that your
self-concept is an accurate reflection of your true potential,
and not simply a reflection of what you have achieved so far.
You make yourself a victim of your autobiography *to date*.

Now, the sceptic might ask, 'How can I be sure that
a person's self-concept does act to limit development?
Perhaps, the person really has reached his or her limits?'
Well, one reason why this is probably not so is the rules that
people live by in playing the game of 'Statues'. The rules are
straightforward:

> 1. Wherever possible avoid appearing ignorant or at a
> loss (if necessary, bluff, etc. – don't say 'I don't know').
> 2. Wherever possible avoid appearing to make mistakes.
> (Even pay the price of never trying anything new in case
> you fail!)
> 3. If you are seen to be ignorant, at a loss or making
> mistakes, panic, feel bad and stop – and interpret the
> ignorance and making of mistakes as proof of little or
> no ability and so call it a day (and, in turn, a lifetime!).

This may be exaggerating a little – but not that much.
Notice your own reaction to the word 'mistake' – 'Oh, I'm
terribly sorry, I've made a mistake'; or 'We don't pay people
to make mistakes'. It's not a word to be used lightly. And
most learning and development, of course, *requires* people

temporarily to be at a loss and to make and eliminate mistakes. 'Only fools never appear foolish.' But for many of us the word 'mistake' is a turn-off and the idea of making mistakes makes us anxious. The anxious person 'spends a part of his task time doing things which are not task oriented. He worries about his performance, worries about how well others might do, ruminates over choices open to him, and is often repetitive in his attempts to solve the task.'[14]

Once we have picked up a mind-set that we may not be good at something, we begin to notice our failures faster than our successes.[15] Likewise if those you work with see you in a negative light it can be extremely difficult to break their mind-set.

Imagine an employer, Mr Smith, who takes on a new employee, Mr Jones. For whatever reason Mr Smith develops a negative set about the employee. Mr Smith needs to delegate work to Mr Jones. The tasks delegated may be brand new for Mr Jones. Mr Smith has executed the task hundreds of times and it is very unlikely that Mr Jones will achieve the same standard first time round. In fact, Mr Jones carries out the task moderately well. However Mr Smith's negative set results in his being fast to detect weaknesses in Mr Jones' performance. The mind-set is contagious and may increase any anxiety Mr Jones had about the task and also reduce enjoyment for that task. Mr Jones begins to notice the difficulties he is having and is comparatively slow to notice his successes. He may, understandably, try to avoid the task and so remain at his original level of competence. Mr Smith's prophecy, therefore, becomes real for himself and for Mr Jones.

Negative prophecies about our children, ourselves and others are probably the greatest strait-jacket on human potential. In recognising the constraint we can begin, perhaps, to overthrow it.

> Many, if not most, are the prisoners of their own perceptions of self . . . Vast numbers of people believe they are able to do far less than they really can. As a result they remain chained to unhappy, unproductive, and unsatisfying ways of life. Here is a waste of human resources compared with which

our losses in wartime or automobile accidents seem small indeed.[16]

Positive Prophecies

The power of the prophecy is probably most often seen in its negative form. Can't, can't, can't and such related cant. Positive expectations create positive performance. But then as a parent, teacher and manager comes the question of how to deal with mistakes. Even though the making and eliminating of mistakes lies at the heart of much learning, surely you have sometimes to be able to alert those learning to when a mistake is made. Otherwise you will praise them endlessly while they foul up magnificently!

Learn to apply the '3 to 1' or '3 to 2' philosophy – that is, whenever you correct someone, tell that person three good things about the way they are performing the task to every one criticism you make. The more robust the other person's self-concept and/or their knowledge of your unconditional faith in them and their ability, the more you can move to three compliments to two criticisms or even one to one. However, as always, everyone is different, so you have to check and see. Do, however, start on the ratio of three compliments to one criticism. Otherwise you run the risk of giving to the other a negative set about themselves and making them anxious. The learner may also stop listening to you because you are hitting the 'hottest planet' – the ego!

Exactly the same principle applies to your own learning and development – acknowledge your progress and success whilst eliminating your mistakes. And providing you learn from your mistakes, the more mistakes you make the faster you learn.

'All very well.' says the sceptic, 'In the meantime your learner could have created havoc in my organisation.' This is, as usual, an insightful 'yes . . . but'. When it comes to people development, some very large organisations adopt the policy of 'drop them in it and let them sink or swim'. For example, an individual may be taken from one function and simply dropped into a new one. There will usually be enough other people in the function who can 'carry' the newcomer during the learning period. If he masters one area, it is probably time to drop him in it again!

The dangers of this formula are twofold. As our sceptic points out, in a company where there is no safety in numbers, mistakes matter; there is the risk of organisational damage. One solution is the development of job descriptions which are divided into two parts – 'expected performance' and 'expected learning'. The 'expected learning' part outlines qualities of skill, attitude and knowledge which are expected at the *next* level or in the next job. The 'expected performance' part is like a conventional job description. What was 'expected learning' in the last job is 'expected performance' in the new.

The second problem of the 'sink or swim' policy is psychological. The learner may be a player of statues, become anxious, self-doubting and so fall prey to a negative prophecy.

The Success – Failure Profile

Along with adopting the 3:1 compliments/criticism rule, understanding the 'Success Profile' and practising it on yourself and others will encourage fast and efficient learning. Adoption of the 'success' end of the success – failure scale – in the way you think about yourself as a learner and the way you treat others – can dramatically increase the rate of your own, your colleagues' and family's development.[17]

0	5	10
Failure		Success

Think of success/failure on a scale between 0 (outright failure) and 10 (brilliant success). As with most scales, few people live right at either end. Furthermore people sit at different points on the scale for different areas of learning and development. For example, you may have a failure profile of 1 for learning a foreign language and a success profile as high as 8 when it comes to playing tennis.

Obviously, a high scorer can succeed or fail in any given task, just like a low scorer. The difference between the two types lies in how they *attribute* their ups and downs, their successes and failures or mistakes.

Faced with a failure or mistake, the high scorer on the scale, that is the person with the success profile, reasons as follows (also see Figure 6.1):

(a) 'You can't win them all.' For example, the salesman who fails to close one particular sale can sometimes quite reasonably say this. (If, however, people keep failing to 'close' and, in turn, continue to use this attribution, they are over-protecting themselves by not understanding what it is they are doing wrong and then changing their behaviour in the light of this understanding.)

(b) 'This is a skill yet to be developed or to be developed further.' For example, when you start to speak another language, you don't expect instant competence. Likewise, the first public speech you give that doesn't go completely to plan. Unfortunately many adults simply fail to work on this understanding. It is as though many of us, if asked the questions 'Are you a good software designer?' 'Are you a good heart surgeon?' 'Are you a good philosopher?' reply 'No', when a reply closer to the truth is: 'If I really wanted to be one of those things, I could probably be, at least, quite good – if anything, very good.' We 'British', however, seem to assume that to boast competence is to be arrogant. True enough, bragging arrogance is unattractive. Here, we are discussing the opposite. Those who brag are, in fact, unsure about their abilities – which is why, of course, they have to brag, in the hope that in convincing others, they may even convince themselves. What is being acknowledged, therefore is the opposite of arrogance. All of us are hugely able – and there is every reason why we feel we can celebrate, nurture and manifest this potential.

(c) 'Insufficient time/effort has been invested in this project.' For example, if you rush to complete an assignment, any mistakes can appropriately be put down to lack of time and not any supposed lack of innate ability.

Faced with success, the person with the success profile attributes success to himself, in that he or she says that if you work hard enough, in the right way, you can get on top of most things.

Faced with failure, the low scorer on the scale, that is the person with the failure profile, attributes the failure entirely to himself: 'You've either got it or you haven't – I haven't' – and so gives up. There is an underlying assumption of a fairly low and fixed level of competence – God-given or genetic competence – or rather, incompetence.

Some people may derive support for this limiting position through noticing that certain people develop faster than others in developing certain skills. Speed of learning and development is clearly affected by a range of interacting factors – motivation, anxiety, selecting the 'appropriate way of learning', existing knowledge and skills which can accelerate or hinder the new learning (for example, old knowledge or skill can interfere with new learning – so there may be a need to break down the old mind-set, or 'unlearn' before learning). In other words, there are very real background differences between people which will affect how quickly they learn and develop. But from school onwards we misinterpret such differences. We believe that fast means bright and slow means stupid. No! No! No! Fast means you've caught the ert of the individual and found the way they like to learn. Slow may mean the opposite and even if the person is slower (and we are all slower than the *one* fastest), speed of learning tells us about preferred speed of learning and not about learning potential. Yet, so often we depress and limit ourselves by believing that speed reflects underlying potential.

Confronted and perhaps even surprised by success, the person with the failure profile attributes the success to factors which leave his or her self-concept fixed and limited: 'What a fluke – beginner's luck,' or, 'Any old fool could have managed that – it was so easy.'

And so the individual with the success profile is prepared to try and try and try – almost *ad nauseam*. Furthermore such success types need not be demotivated or undermined in the case of failure.

The failure profile, at best, may try once, and given any difficulty is then likely to stop. One irony is, therefore, that

Figure 6.1   Success and Failure Profile

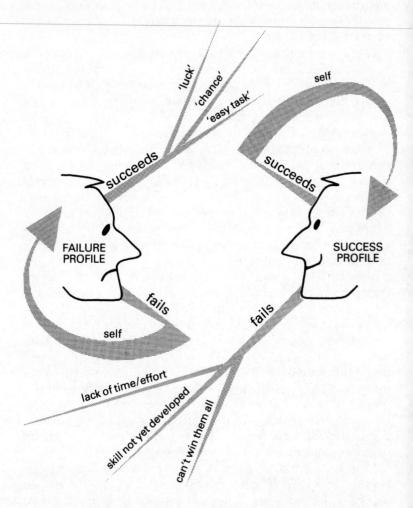

even if you buy into the old-world assumption that we have limited potential, and some more than others, the attributions we make may enable the person with supposedly less potential easily to outperform the other with the supposed greater potential!

Clearly the success – failure profile applies to the way we treat others. So along with the 3:1 balance of compliments to criticisms, you can communicate the underlying philosophy of the success profile in a range of ways:

> – 'OK, so it didn't go so well, but it's the first time you tried. You can't ride a bike first go.'
> – 'My first go went just like that. I just got the hang of it by working at it. You will too.'
> – Or even – and although this sounds a bit extreme, perhaps harsh, the underlying message is still an acknowledgement of potential: 'The reason why you failed is simple enough – you didn't put enough work into it.'

And in the case of successful learning or achievement:

> – 'It just goes to show the potential you have. Do you remember when you felt unsure if you could ever do this? Just imagine what else you could do, if you want to, that is.'
> – 'Whatever you put your mind to, you can do, can't you?'

Therefore beware pushing others down the failure end by unduly crediting their successes to luck, the ease of the task, or yourself! The pressures of work may make it all too easy 'to manage by exception'. Doing this stifles and does not nurture potential.

Lastly, think about your own potential. There will be areas of potential competence which you know you can acquire – that is, you already have the success profile. There will be other areas of potential competence, which at this point are not even 'potential' because you believe you cannot master them – you have a perfect failure profile. Is it not time to recognise and start to challenge such a failure profile in yourself – and others?

Competencies I Might Live to Develop

Success profile areas	'Failure' profile areas
_____	_____
_____	_____
_____	_____
_____	_____
_____	_____
_____	_____
_____	_____
_____	_____
_____	_____

Management Learning and Development

Part of ensuring your organisation's success lies in having people equipped with strategically determined behaviours, knowledge and attitudes that enable you to succeed in the market-place. Part of this responsibility falls to those looking after human resource development (HRD).

'HRD' or management development and particularly 'training' (what we usually do with performing seals!) in many

organisations is seen as a joke. And a joke it is. Certainly, with
some major exceptions, my overriding impression of most
'in-house' training functions, over some fifteen years, is far
from favourable. You only have to look at what happens to the
training and development budget if cut-backs are necessary
– it is often the first budget to go.

Furthermore, in many organisations it pays to have a look
at the status and credibility of trainers. Are these the heroes
of the organisation – or struggling line managers who have a
couple of years' training?

Put simply we need to develop people – and either we
should do it effectively or not do it at all. For a range of
reasons, most organisations are, at best, ineffective.

One estimate, which may well now be surpassed, put
the investment in training/education/development for one
year in the US at:

> . . .well over $100 billion. Unfortunately, most evalu-
> ations of training find little measurable behavioral
> change on the job. Studies on the long-range ef-
> fects of training show, in most cases, no significant
> difference following training in the occurrence of
> those organizational problems which the training
> was designed to improve.[18]

Following a learning intervention, like a course, some people's performance may actually decline! An individual's old
but moderately efficient way of doing things may be unsettled
through the introduction of a better way. However, if the new
way is insufficiently reinforced and so interferes with the old
way of doing things, it actually reduces the prior level of
moderate competence! Not only is much 'training' having a
marginal impact, some of it is making things worse!

So where are the problems? First of all drop the word 'training' – humans are not rats you train to run through mazes.
The word 'training' may also carry the connotation that you
can 'learn' people. Secondly, think and work through the
following hurdles to effective learning and development.
(David Georgenson's work has proved influential here.)[19]

Profit-Related Behaviours

Are learning objectives derived in the light of your strategy? In other words, if you are a commercial organisation, are you identifying profit-related behaviours, skills and attitudes? That is, what changes do you want in whom, by when, concerning what behaviours/knowledge/attitudes, so as to achieve your strategic goals? In the non-commercial sector, terms like 'core or critical competences' may be appropriate.

Sadly what happens in many organisations is that HR or trainers ask a cross-section of managers what 'training' they would like *for* their people. This is therefore a non-collaborative process for those to be 'trained' and many managers will come up with the flavour of the month/ year or decade: 'Oh, assertiveness training and "situational leadership" sound great fun,' etc. The same manager, the following year may be asking for 'sensitivity training' as he now finds that many of his people have become 'too assertive'. In the meantime none of the new learning may be relevant to organisational performance.

Remedial, Developmental and Strategically Relevant Learning

'Remedial' learning is straightforward. If I'm missing a necessary skill which I should have picked up but haven't, some help is appropriate. The more difficult question is what is the balance and overlap between learning which is for the individual's sake and learning which supports strategy.

For example, do you expect all development to be in pursuit of organisational goals, at least ultimately – as illustrated in Figure 6.2? Or are you prepared to develop the individual for his or her own sake, even if this has nothing to do with the organisation's short-term welfare and may, in fact, encourage that person to look outside your organisation for their next job – Figure 6.3? Or do you aim for both – Figure 6.4? In which case, how large is the area of overlap you want? These are again questions of your 'shared values'.

Figure 6.2

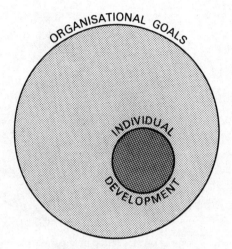

individual developed only in
context of organisational goals

Figure 6.3

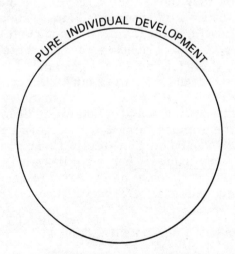

prepared to develop the individual
even though no overlap with organisational goals

Figure 6.4

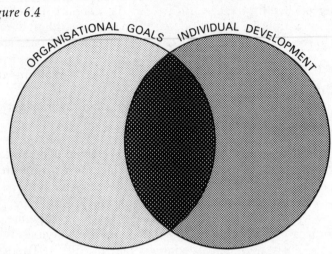

expect some overlap between
organisational & personal development

Motivated, Relevant and Supported Learning

Unless people are involved in thinking through their own development, they cannot be expected to be motivated by the idea of some course or seminar. Many seminars are seen as a fringe benefit, in the form of fun along with a couple of days off. People must be able to see the relevance of material in the light of organisational and personal objectives. The learning content and objectives must also be seen to be relevant by the learner's colleagues, so that they encourage him to put his newly acquired or improved skill into practice. Otherwise the learner returns to the work-place only to face an attitude of 'Don't mind him – he's just been on a course!' In other words, any change in behaviour is seen as a temporary aberration which will pass shortly. And it usually does. The new skill often fails to transfer back to the work-place.

Appropriate Learning Content and Style

And this, of course, assumes that the content is worth transferring back to work in the first place. There is an excess of alluring concepts and management tricks which have little pedigree, just high face validity. That is, the material may at least look superficially sound. And although my intent here is not to set about sabotaging various concepts and packages, people are well advised to spend a little more time ensuring the 'rigor' of different ideas, while perhaps, avoiding the 'mortis' of becoming too academic!

Assuming that the content is sound, many managers fail to really 'get' the message/s put across. And whereas in the past, 'trainers' might have labelled such managers as dullards or demotivated, the problem is often one of context or 'thinking style'. Methods and materials for learning must be geared to match the increased knowledge we now have about people's preferred styles and pace of learning. If people are very concrete learners, make the learning concrete. If learners are conceptual and abstract in their style, adjust accordingly – if practical, enable them to 'do' it. There is never a stupid learner, just 'teachers' or facilitators who are stuck in their own world and style – never stupid learners – only stupid teachers. If you can select a group so that they have a shared style of learning, life can be easier than if styles are mixed. Mixed styles will mean that a course has to be designed so that there are a variety of learning mechanisms available at critical learning points.[20]

The New and Old Model of Mind

Most training is underpinned by the 'Old Model of Mind' (see Figure 6.5). At its most naive the Old Model predicts that once we have understood a principle, technique etc., we will subsequently apply it where appropriate. It is assumed that understanding gives rise to the expected behavioural change. Although this is clearly possible and does happen sometimes, we greatly overestimate the extent to which this takes place.

Many 'trainers' like to make a distinction between *task* and *process*. For example, the task of a seminar could involve the building of a 'Lego' tower or abseiling down a cliff and the processes being studied could be communication and team building skills respectively. This separation of task from process/skill is often an excellent way to help managers

Figure 6.5   Old Model of Mind

Assumption – can separate process and task.
True for awareness purposes
False for learning purposes

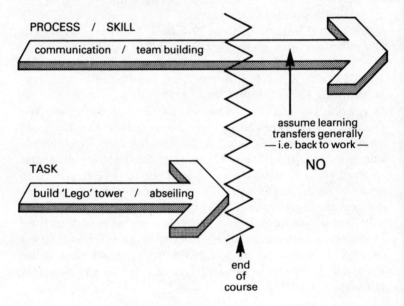

become aware of the process under scrutiny. If you keep too close to the work context a manager may remain fixated on the task and fail to notice the process. The artificial task helps separate out the process. And, as shown, the old model assumes that at the end of the course, the new skill transfers back to the work-place. The model assumes that the course will help the learner along some 95 per cent of the total learning journey. This assumption is false.

The New Model of Mind is depicted in Figure 6.6. This model realises that understanding is obviously important before any individual sees the relevance of why a behaviour should be taken on board. However, it predicts that the manager who has learnt about communication skills in the situation of building a 'Lego' tower, will use those new or improved skills only – if at all – on those occasions when he or she is subsequently building another such or very similar

Figure 6.6   New Model of Mind

Assumptions - can separate process and task for awareness purposes.
CANNOT separate process and task for learning purposes

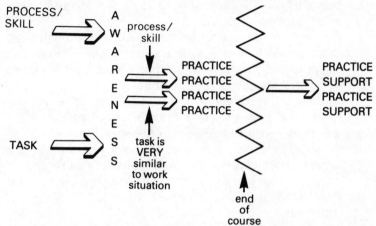

tower! Likewise the team skills may re-emerge when you
are next abseiling down the side of a cliff. Whereas the Old
Model assumes that the skill and the situation within which
that skill is learnt are separable (true for awareness purposes)
so that the skill will transfer generally to a range of situa-
tions/tasks, the New Model makes a different prediction.
The New says that what you do and perceive as successful
in one situation, you are likely to do again in the same or a
very similar situation. So that if you want learning to transfer
back to the work-place, the new skill/knowledge/attitude
has to be practised, practised and practised in a situation
which is very similar to the work situation (i.e. simulations
during a course) and practised and reinforced back at work.
Skill and task/situation are inseparable.

However the New Model poses some interesting problems.
The idea that understanding of a principle or skill does not
necessarily give rise to 'transfer' of that skill seems an affront
to intelligence. But think of just one practical situation –
the car-skid. I may completely understand the principle of
what to do in a skid but fail totally to apply it at the critical
moment. Secondly, 'trainers' may resist the idea of really
practising the newly acquired skill with course delegates
during a course, because:

1. Although the delegates have gone along with the fun of the original 'awareness' exercise – tower-building, business games and the like – their enthusiasm may begin to wane if they have to apply what may be seen as an unimportant skill.

2. Some delegates may be mismatched in their jobs so that getting close to work in the form of simulations and the practising of the new skill may smack a bit too much of the real and depressing world.

3. Some trainers rely on the instant froth of various awareness games to achieve their 'clapometer' scores – i.e. 'How much did you enjoy the jaunt?' In all fairness to many trainers, they may be set up to fail, as the organisation, especially at senior levels, may be simply paying lip-service to the idea of developing their people (how many top managers are seen on 'in-company' courses?).

The New Model predicts that a course can only provide an opportunity for 5 per cent of the total required practice. The rest of the 95 per cent practice necessary for achieving complete competence has to take place in the work context. And unless the whole developmental activity is seen as strategically and personally relevant there is no way colleagues and managers will support the learner in acquiring mastery. The vicious circle will have continued.

Tested and Modified Learning

Seminars, workshops and the like need to be evaluated to check that the seminar was appreciated (clapometer), that the skill/knowledge/attitude is being applied appropriately and that this skill/knowledge/attitude is helping achieve the specified functional/organisational goal (i.e. in commercial organisations, that the behaviour really is a profit-related one). Modification follows accordingly.

In other words, people are the greatest resource. So develop people properly or don't do it at all. Otherwise you create justifiable scepticism about development programmes as being a fringe benefit, etc. This results in low motivation for those attending courses and no effective transfer of appropriate skills.

The above discussion of management development assumes that you are developing the individual in the direction that he or she wants as well as that which the organisation wishes. This therefore raises what is for many the trickiest question of them all. Where do you want to develop? Where do you wish to get to? What are your goals? And here is the real difficulty, 'The reason most do not achieve their heart's desire is because they don't know what it is.' Hence the next chapter.

References

1. See, for example: Russell, P. *The Brain Book*, Hawthorn Books, 1979.
   Walmsley, J. & Margolis, J. *Hot House People*, Pan Books, 1987.
2. Holt, J. *How Children Fail*, Sir Issac Pitman & Sons Ltd., 1964, p.167.
3. Wagar, W. W. *The City of Man*, Houghton Mifflin, 1963, p.66.
4. Allport, G. W. 'The Role of Expectancy.' in *Tensions that Cause Wars*, Cantril, H. (Ed.) University of Illinois Press, 1950, p.179.
5. Rosenthal, R. & Jacobson, L. *Pygmalion in the Classroom*, Holt, Rinehart and Winston, 1968, p.38.
6. Rosenthal, R. & Jacobson, L. Ibid. p.6.
7. Rosenthal, R. & Jacobson, L. Ibid. p.6.
8. Rosenthal, R. & Jacobson, L. Ibid.
9. Rosenthal, R. & Jacobson, L. 'Teacher Expectations for the Disadvantaged.' *Scientific American*, April 1968, Volume 218, Number 4, p.22.
10. 'Pygmalion Revisited.' *Brain Mind Bulletin*, April 1988, Volume 13, Number 7, p.1 and see, *Journal of Educational Psychology*, 79, pp.461–466.
11. Eden, D. & Shani, A. B. 'Pygmalion goes to boot camp: expectancy, leadership, and trainee performance.' *Journal of Applied Psychology*, 1982, Vol. 67, No. 2, pp.194–199.
12. Eden, D. & Shani, A. B. Ibid. p.194.
13. Eden, D. & Shani, A. B. Ibid. p.197.
14. Marlett, N. J. & Watson, D. 'Test anxiety and immediate or delayed feedback in a test-like avoidance task.' *Journal of Personality and Social Psychology*, 1968, 8, p.203.

15. Postman, L. & Brown, D. R. 'The perceptual consequences of success and failure.' *Journal of Abnormal and Social Psychology*, 1952, 47, pp.213–221.

16. Combs, A. W., Richards, A. H. & Richards, F. *Perceptual Psychology*, Harper & Row, 1976, p.185.

17. The different ways in which people attribute and make sense of success, failure and other events in their lives lies at the heart of Attribution Theory.
    See, for example: Antaki, C. & Brewin, C. (Eds.) *Attributions and Psychological Change*, Academic Press, 1982.

18. Broad, M. L. 'Management actions to support transfer of training.' *Training and Development Journal*, May, 1982, p.124.

19. Georgenson, D. L. 'The problem of transfer calls for partnership.' *Training and Development Journal*, October, 1982, pp.75–78.

20. See: Kolb, D. A. *Experiential Learning*, Prentice Hall, 1984.
    Kolb, D. A., Rubin, I. M. & McIntyre, J. M. (Eds.) *Organizational Psychology, readings on human behavior in organizations*, Prentice-Hall, fourth edition, 1984.
    Kolb, D. A., Rubin, I. M. & McIntyre, J. M. (Eds.) *Organizational Psychology, an experiential approach to organizational behavior*, Prentice-Hall, fourth edition, 1984.
    Kolb's Learning-Style Inventory can be purchased from:
    McBer and Company,
    137 Newbury Street,
    Boston,
    Massachusetts 02116
    USA
    Tel (617) 437-7080
    And see:
    Honey, P. & Mumford, A. *The Manual of Learning Styles*, 1982.
    Honey, P. & Mumford, A. *Using Your Learning Styles*, 1983.
    Both published by:
    Peter Honey,
    Ardingly House,
    10, Linden Avenue,
    Maidenhead,
    Berkshire SL6 6HB
    England

CHAPTER SEVEN

Going Places
that Really Suit You

Grid Tension

A simple starting-point for seeing where you want to go is
the original judgement grid you filled in at the back of the
book. Simply place an X on each scale which represents
how you see yourself now. (If the scale is irrelevant to you,
skip it.) Now place a different mark, say an 'O', for where
you would like to be. If your X's coincide with your O's,
you are already an extraordinarily happy person! However,
for us lesser mortals (and perhaps a degree of dissatisfaction
or tension proves to be the essential grit in the oyster) there
will normally be some mismatch. What ideas come to mind
as to how to close the gap?

Now it may be that your job is already helping close the
gap, or perhaps, increasing it! To find out, put a third and
final mark, say a small box, on the scale which represents
how you feel you are 'meant to be' in your job – that is how
you feel your boss or the 'organisation' wants you to be. The
picture now comes a little clearer. Your job may be keeping
you at your present level of satisfaction/dissatisfaction – or
reducing or increasing that level. For example, you might
have rated a scale 'freedom – conformity' and find that *you*
want more freedom but you think your job requires you to

conform. On the other hand, on another scale you may have 'risk – security' (and assume here you like a high level of security) and find that there is a good match between where you are, where you want to be and where the organisation allows you to be. So your desire as seen on one scale may contradict your intention expressed on another. (That is, in this example you could jeopodise your job security by pushing for too much freedom!) Such contradictions reveal the different parts of ourselves, or if you like, the various smaller characters who combine to create the total character – 'you'. And, as we all know, keeping any group of people happy all the time can be quite a task – be those people outside or inside us! We will return to this 'multiple character' issue towards the end of the chapter.

No Limits

Let's get another possible bearing on what you want in life. This 'Do, Be, Have' exercise can be fun to do, as well as giving you some helpful insights. All you have to do is forget about the 'real' world and jot down everything that you would like to *do, be* and *have* – if there were no limits whatsoever. This therefore allows you to state mutually exclusive goals (i.e. be successful in business, be a monk). Remember it is *everything* that you would possibly like to be, do and have and there are absolutely no limits. So let your imagination run riot!

Do, Be, Have Chart

Jot down everything that you would like to be, do and have

_____

_____

_____

_____

Now circle each and every idea which is *possible* for you
to achieve, where possible means *not impossible*. Treat each
idea in isolation in doing this. In other words, you needn't,
at this point concern yourself with any contradictions. Very
few of the ideas will be impossible. That is, very few of the
ideas sit right at absolute zero on the scale below. They may
be scoring 1, 2 or 3 but rarely zero. Becoming a 100 metre
Olympic Gold medallist, when you are now turning seventy,
may be pushing it a bit – but most of your ideas will be
possible. They may be very unlikely, but they are possible.

Likelihood of things being achieved

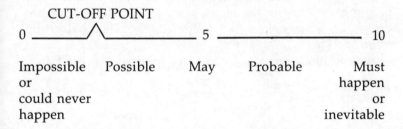

CUT-OFF POINT

0		5		10
Impossible	Possible	May	Probable	Must
or				happen
could never				or
happen				inevitable

Possible they may be, you agree, but this is not enough for
you to have a go at reaching out towards these pipe-dreams.
This is because 'hopefulness is a precondition for action'.[1]
We are unlikely to set out on a journey unless we feel that we
want to go in the first place *and* that there is a fair chance of
getting to our destination. Thus there are the two ingredients
of 'desire' and 'perceived probability of success'. If we do
not strongly desire the idea and it is only 'possible' that we
may get there anyway, we may well decide to stay at home.
This all seems quite sensible.

If Only

Every one of us has our own unique cut-off point on the scale of possibility. The more an idea tends towards zero, the greater the chance you will *not* consider it seriously. Somewhere on the scale is your own particular cut-off point – and if an idea is below that point, you will dream about it – but only dream about it; if the idea sits above that point you may get on and do something about it. (Whether or not you actually get on with a goal you do feel sufficiently hopeful about achieving will be a question of what else you are doing and how much you desire that goal.)

Now here comes Catch 22. Take the arrow in Figure 7.1 to represent the flow of time. Ideas or fantasies that live below our cut-off point remain as pure pipe-dreams. All of us have these *vague* dreams – 'wouldn't it be great if etc'. With *vague* goals we notice opportunities, if at all, that would *have* enabled us to move towards them, but only once the opportunities have passed. Thus we come up with the classic 'If . . . only' remark.

Louis Pasteur said that 'Chance favours only the prepared mind.' And chance with its variety of opportunities and openings will favour the *prepared* mind. But *vague* goals are not sufficient to create that preparedness. The goal needs to be *specific*.

Imagine that you and I conspire together to rob a bank.

Figure 7.1   The Opportunity Arrow

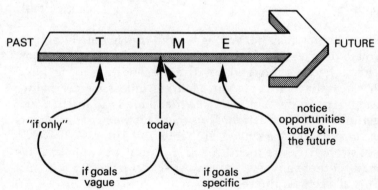

So we have changed a perhaps *vague* goal of 'Wouldn't it be fun to be very wealthy' to a specific one of 'We are going to rob a bank'. From the moment of that decision onwards we become sensitised to any relevant information that moves us towards fulfilling our (hypothetical, I hope (!)) goal. Even when we go into a bank for normal (non-criminal) purposes we find ourselves alerted to numerous aspects of security, lay-out, types of transactions, etc.

Once a goal becomes specific, you start to notice pathways towards the attainment of that goal. You begin to construe the world differently. Whereas, before, your world may have been full of large flashing No's, now the Yes's become visible. You, therefore, become more hopeful about being able to achieve it. On the other hand, if the goal remains vague, you notice opportunities when they are past and thus remain insufficiently hopeful or confident to consider attempting it.

I am not saying that once a dream climbs past your cut-off point you will decide to aim for it as an actual goal. What I'm saying is that such a goal will not be considered at all unless you can shift it beyond that cut-off point. Once beyond that point you may or may not aim for it and you may or may not achieve it. But what is certain is that as long as it remains below the 'hopefulness' cut-off point, nothing at all will happen. In other words, the way we construe our world limits the number of choices open to us. In realising that we do construe our world, we can begin to consider construing it in different and more satisfying ways.

Planning Backwards

This exercise helps move most, if not all, of your pipe-dream ideas beyond the cut-off point. Whereas before you could

IDEA 1

today		week 1	
CALL STEPHEN & DISCUSS HOW HE GOT HIS FIRST BOOK PUBLISHED. CONTACT 'SOCIETY OF AUTHORS'. START WRITING FOR BETWEEN 1 & 2 HOURS A DAY. THINK THROUGH WHEN I WRITE BEST — MORNINGS/ EVENING. DECIDE HOW TO PLAN EXISTING WORK SO AS TO HELP GET THIS BOOK WRITTEN.		DRAFT OUTLINE ALONG WITH CHAPTER 1. BUY 'WRITERS & ARTISTS' YEARBOOK. CHECK IF THERE ARE OTHER BOOKS ON WRITING & GETTING PUBLISHED. HAVE A LOOK AT CHEAP BUT EFFECTIVE WORDPROCESSORS/ TYPEWRITERS.	
month 1	month 3	month 6	month 9
SEND OUTLINE & WAIT! START WRITING THE BOOK — MINIMUM OF A CHAPTER A MONTH.	3 CHAPTERS COMPLETE.	6 CHAPTERS COMPLETE.	9 CHAPTERS COMPLETE.

week 2	week 3
DRAW UP LIST OF POSSIBLE PUBLISHERS. PRODUCE SHORTLIST. REDRAFT OUTLINE AND CHAPTER 1.	COMPLETE DRAFT AND CHAPTER 1. ASK ONE OR TWO FRIENDS FOR CRITICISM.

year 1	year 2	year 3	year 4	year 5
BOOK FINISHED & REREAD. S C R I P T COMPLETE & ACCEPTED.	P U B L I C A T I O N			

In this example the completed goal is entered in the 2 year column as this was the 'guess' as to how long the project might take.

DECISION: 1 — YES!

IDEA 1

today		week 1	
month 1	month 3	month 6	month 9

week 2		week 3		

year 1	year 2	year 3	year 4	year 5

DECISION:

not exercise choice and decide whether or not the goal was worth the required effort, you will now be in that position.

Take an idea from the 'Do, Be, Have' chart which is not impossible and that also interests you. It's probably one of those ideas which has fascinated you for some considerable time. Start by guessing how long it might take you to achieve the goal. Put the *achieved goal* in the appropriate column in the chart below – for example, if you think the goal will take three years to achieve, put it in the 3 year column. Now work out what you will have had to achieve by when so as to enable you to reach that goal. As far as possible specify *an exact imaginary route* which results in the achievement of the goal. Fill in each and every column through to today, explaining a route to the achievement of the goal. Whether or not you finally go for the goal and whether the route taken follows the one specified here are secondary issues.

What you will find happening as you go through the backward planning exercise on every 'Do, Be, Have' idea which interests you is that each idea will turn into one of three things:

1. *Yes* . . . which simply means that you are now sufficiently hopeful that you want to attempt the specific goal. As it is specific there will be a variety of opportunities you become sensitised to. If you've decided to write a book, you'll find yourself more aware of the people you know and meet who write, relevant displays in bookshops and the like. So you start moving in the direction of the goal. The planning exercise therefore launches you into action. Again, I stress that the route you follow may not be the one planned. You may land up as a journalist instead, but at least you broke the hypnotic spell born of the sense of hopelessness and a world full of flashing 'No's'.

2. *Not me Superperson* (or if you prefer, 'Can I have my halo back?'). Here, having done the plan, you realise that the idea is a form of 'psychological baggage' which has been weighing you down for years. You never really wanted to do this anyway, at all. However you have always felt that you 'should' or 'ought' to try to achieve this. Perhaps the largest 'should' is the one which says we should be

successful, where success comes pre-defined and may have little or nothing to do with our deeper aspirations. Numerous ideals which plague us can be subtly dumped on us from early childhood on, by family, friends, our society and culture. The media is one obvious source of influence which promotes a subtle and powerful image of how people 'should' be – high-budget American soap operas are amongst the more blatant of examples.

And because we have these 'ideals', we may feel less OK about ourselves than if we didn't have them. Thus we give away our sense of being OK – we give away our own halos. By realising that many of these 'should' ideals are not for you anyway, you can give the halo back – to yourself.

3. *Desire/priorities.* In this case, as in *Yes . . .* you realise that you can probably achieve the goal but – either there are too many other demanding or conflicting activities or you are not prepared to invest the effort required to achieve the goal. Of course, you can consider whether there isn't a smarter or more ingenious way of achieving your goal in the first place so that effort is reduced.

However, beware! Many of us may use the plea of 'Yes I can – but my commitments, the family, the mortgage . . .' whilst forgetting that ultimately we *choose* these commitments. 'Yes, but,' says the sceptic, 'you can hardly expect me to throw caution to the wind and start a new career.' Well, the point to ponder is what happens to adults if they spend years trapped in a life that doesn't suit them. How does this rub off on the family and friends? Would not the family, perhaps, prefer the individual who is alive and vibrant – the person who is 'matched' to his or her work life?

The Do, Be, Have Triangle[2]

There is a danger with what has been outlined and explored so far. Such goal-setting and planning exercises may be built up on some fairly arbitrary and ultimately unhelpful assumptions. These particular assumptions can be difficult to spot because they are shared by many of us.

The first is an extension of 'not me Superperson'. It's fine to aim 'to be successful' if that's what *you* really want. It's equally all right *not* to be successful. Sadly our goals often turn out to be cover-ups for aspects of ourselves which we are not comfortable with. For example, a person who feels little-recognised may set himself – and even achieve – grandiose goals, only to find that with failing eyesight and a dicky heart he has achieved what he thought was important but has, in fact, not tackled the basic problem at all. Time would have been better spent in that person winning his own good regard as opposed to trying to achieve it indirectly. Marilyn Monroe and others epitomise the error of trusting to others to put right our own inner wounds. Such wounds need direct attention and perhaps the hardest lesson to learn in life is that we are in fact fine the way we are. We do not have to make our sense of value dependent on the achievement of external goals and other people's fleeting approval and acknowledgement.

The sceptic could argue, at this point, that the world of thrusting achievement would not exist if it were not for all those folk trying (unsuccessfully) to solve internal issues through achieving external goals (sometimes successfully). I guess the sceptic could well be right. Psychological distress, in part, makes the world go round.

Furthermore, our society encourages people to define their lives in terms of what they do and what they have. 'What do you do?' and 'Where do you live/What do you drive?' So, in terms of a 'Do, Be, Have Triangle', the emphasis runs from determining what you want to have, and therefore what you need to do – and these two may be out of line with who we 'be' or are. 'Do', of course, may precede 'Have'. All the same, 'Be' often comes last.

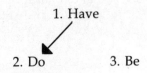

1. Have

2. Do   3. Be

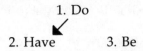

The result is often that people feel misaligned. That is, their deep 'ert' is not matched to what they are doing in the world. If, however, we change the apex of the triangle,

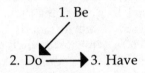

so that 'Be' determines 'Do' and 'Do' determines 'Have', life looks somewhat different. First of all the individual remains 'truer' to him or herself (the word 'truer' warrants another book in itself). Secondly what the person does is so in tune with their ert that the level of enthusiasm and intrinsic satisfaction is very high – work becomes play – and hard 'play' and enthusiasm often create adequate if not an abundance of reward.

Lastly there is the danger that too strong a goal-orientation results in a failure to live the only life we have – and that life is *now*. For example, if I decide that life is perfect at those moments when I have just swallowed a mouthful of champagne, my teeth are sinking into a succulent strawberry and my eyes are wandering over a perfectly still Caribbean sunset, then I am setting myself up *not* to enjoy all the other moments – that is practically all the time. The trick is to enjoy the process of being and not just the rare and fleeting moment of arriving. '. . . unless one is able to live fully in the present, the future is a hoax . . .'[3]

Multiple Characters

So, practically, how can we tie the 'No Limits' and the backward-planning exercises in with the aim of acknowledging who you are or 'be', rather than being excessively driven by what you want. How do you get a healthy balance and not a misalignment between the different forces within you?

These different forces have been referred to as the different characters or 'sub-personalities' that combine together as a whole to make up who you are. On first hearing this can seem an odd idea and may even have connotations of a 'split personality', but this is not the case. People recognise in everyday life, that there are a range of sub-characters who combine overall to give them their sense of self. For example, you may say 'I feel in conflict about this' or 'A part of me feels'. Here you acknowledge the existence of those different parts.

You can take the idea of 'sub-personalities' one stage further and begin to name and creatively listen to these separate entities. This is done, in part, in Transactional Analysis[4] and in other types of growth psychology/therapy such as 'Voice Dialogue'.[5] Here is an array of some possible characters:

- the critic – that part which is always criticising yourself and others,
- the pusher – that part which is flogging you to get on and achieve,
- the controller – who decides what is and is not OK and which other characters are permissible,
- the playful child – that part which simply wants to play and dance in the sun,
- the sad child – that depressed and withdrawn young person,
- the wise person – that counsellor who if asked, usually has some very sound advice,
- the hater – that part of you which is angry and has to find something to hate or rage against,
- the traditionalist – that part which hankers after the known and the established (who won't like the idea of this exercise at all, perhaps!),
- the rebel – who loathes routine, and at times wants to smash any system or control.

As you have already guessed, each of us has our own unique set of characters. Some we know well, others only occasionally get heard – that is, the Controller may not be too happy with some of the characters.

You can jot down some of the characters you feel go to make up yourself. The list above probably contains some flavour of your characters and you may wish to add more of your own.

_____

_____

_____

_____

_____

_____

_____

_____

What you can now do is go back to the ideas which have been labelled '1 Yes . . .' and ask yourself, 'Which parts of me are being fulfilled/stifled by going for this goal?' – and so consider what you can do to modify the goal so that more parts of you are in agreement. Secondly, take those goals which have been labelled as 3 – that is 'Desire/priorities' and likewise consider how you could alter the goal to suit more parts of you.

Lastly, and most importantly, keep a continuing note of how you feel about the goals you are working on. For example, you may find that you lose interest in a certain goal. This may be telling you that you had over-emphasised the match of that specific goal with parts of yourself – or that there are other parts of yourself which were previously less or not acknowledged which are beginning to reveal themselves. In this way the goal-planning exercise can help you both work on goals which have deep meaning for you and, at the same time, find out more about your whole 'being'. This is therefore one way to keep 'being' in touch and more in tune with 'doing' and 'having'.

References

For anyone who wants to think more about what job to do, I suggest:
Bolles, R. N. *The 1988 What Color is Your Parachute*, Ten Speed Press, 1988.

1. A leading text on self-fulfilling prophecies and how the way in which we construe the world limits what we can choose to do, is: Jones, R. A. *Self-fulfilling Prophecies*, John Wiley, 1977.
2. Some time ago I read an excellent, I believe American, book which helped clarify my ideas on the 'do, be, have' triangle. I would be delighted to hear from any reader who knows the title so that I may reference it in future.
3. Watts, A. *The Book*, Jonathan Cape, 1969, p. 72.
4. See: Berne, E. *Games People Play: The Psychology of Human Relationships*, Grove, 1964.
    Harris, T. A. *I'm OK, You're OK*, Harper & Row, 1967.
5. See: Stone, H. & Winkelman, S. *Embracing Ourselves*, Devorss & Company, 1985.

CHAPTER EIGHT

Ideas into Action

What is all this Talk about Innovation?

> The enterprise that does not innovate inevitably ages and declines. And in a period of rapid change such as the present, an entrepreneurial period, the decline will be fast. (Peter Drucker in *Innovation and Entrepreneurship*.)[1]

Yet:

> . . . one of the collateral purposes of an organization *is* to be inhospitable to a great and constant flow of ideas and creativity. . . . The organization exists to restrict and channel the range of individual actions and behavior into a predictable and knowable routine. Without organization there would be chaos and decay. Organization exists in order to create that amount and kind of inflexibility that are necessary to get the most pressingly intended job done efficiently and on time. (Theodore Levitt in *Harvard Business Review*, 'Creativity is Not Enough'.)[2]

Everyone is talking, writing and consulting about it, running seminars and conferences on it. Innovation, creativity, lateral thinking, change agents, visionaries, entrepreneurs and intrapreneurs (put simply intrapreneurs are entrepreneurs who work within an existing organisation) are all in fashion. But what are people actually doing differently? And how do you capture and stimulate new ideas and translate these into profitable action – whilst continuing to run a productive organisation, free of chaos and anarchy?

Before looking at the question of how to innovate, the sceptic first of all needs to be won over. That is, why all the fuss about innovation? Well the answer is simple enough. Your competitors will do new things and your customers will want better and also new and different products and services. In the end, if you don't innovate, you will not survive. So one reason to innovate is to survive. This is the case of the 'reluctant innovator'. Such individuals and organisations react to change unwillingly – at best.

The obverse of this is that if you want to stay or get ahead of your competitors you must innovate – all the time. This is the 'initiating innovator'. Here people embrace and stimulate productive change – not change for change's sake, but change for the customer's sake and the company's profitability.

The sceptic normally buys into these two reasons. The problem with this whole topic usually revolves around the different interpretations people have of the word 'innovation' itself. Innovation, in the way I and many others use it, does not just mean technological innovation – CD players, digital tape and the like. Innovation applies to products, services and procedures. It encompasses, for example, maintaining and improving quality. One reason for emphasising, in this book, 'innovation' and less so 'quality' is that the latter may primarily suggest bringing standards up to existing levels – and no further. 'Innovation' allows you to include this definition of quality and go beyond it. You can now consider improvements and developments which take you way and beyond the 'normal' standards of quality (see Figure 8.1).

Innovation, therefore, applies to:

- everything your organisation does and could do better;
- everything it does that it shouldn't be doing (check and encourage (!) customer complaints for a taste of what this includes); and
- everything you are not doing that you could successfully be doing.

Figure 8.1   Quality or Innovation?

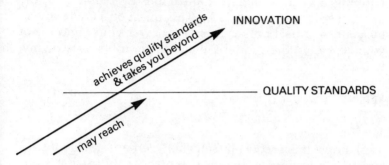

These areas for innovation focus apply equally to commercial and non-commercial organisations.

Therefore areas of potential innovation include:

1. Challenging your existing business definition so as to identify those customers and products/services you most wish to have.
2. Product/service improvement.
3. New products and services.
4. Identifying, attracting and looking after your external and internal customers more effectively.
5. Doing 'whatever' to increase efficiency and/or reduce costs.

In other words, you do whatever it takes to make your existing customer carry on spending money or encouraging new customers to spend money in your favour – or both of these. In the commercial world, the objective of innovation is to keep and/or win customers – profitably. And then to keep doing this – continuously. Innovation is what brings businesses into being in the first place and then keeps them alive and well.

One unanswered question concerns the balance between

winning and satisfying customers and profitability in the short, medium and long term. This question is determined by your organisation's values. The lower your concern for your customer, the shorter the period of profitability, if any, will be.

Why We Don't Innovate

So, I hope the sceptic is satisfied. Perhaps the more interesting question is not 'why innovate?' but 'what stops successful innovation occurring all the time?' Companies originally succeed because they did something that others were not doing. So what happens to that essential and original impetus?

One way of looking at this problem is to consider the way the structure of any system or organism changes. For example, in the case of the human body or human society there is a fine balance between stability and change or renewal. If a system changes too fast it will tend towards chaos and so collapse. If it remains too stable, and in the meantime the world around changes, then in not adapting, it fails to function appropriately. The successful system changes to meet the demands of its environment. A change that is too great may result in the system failing to adapt fast enough. This is apparently what happened to the dinosaur – due to cosmic radiation or the impact of comets, the Earth's temperature apparently changed too quickly for those gigantic lizards to adapt.

The human mind can also be thought of as a system which needs to keep a balance between structure and change. The Swiss biologist and philosopher, Jean Piaget, coined the term 'assimilation' to describe the way that the structures of the mind tend to preserve themselves.[3] The mind attempts to integrate the 'new' within those existing structures. If the change is too great to be organised within them the existing structures change so that the new information can then be successfully absorbed. Piaget coined the term 'accommodation' to describe this structural change. By maintaining some equilibrium between assimilation and accommodation the mind is able to maintain a necessary degree of internal order and yet also adapt itself, over time, to new patterns in the environment. Piaget saw this act of maintaining balance or what he called 'equilibration' as key to the success of the developing child and adult, in a world that constantly changes.

Companies can be seen as having organisational minds. New and successful companies are often energetic and innovative. They may lack a systematic approach. In this sense, they are good at 'accommodating'. But they may not be stable enough. On the other hand, long-standing organisations may have become too structured and have lost much of their original vision, energy and innovation. They are showing a preference for 'assimilating' the new to the old or maybe simply ignoring the new altogether. And if you only keep 'assimilating' in a world of change, there comes a point where your model of the world and behaviour is disastrously out of line with the world 'out there'. This in humans can lead to psychosis. I might begin to believe I am Napoleon. Many organisations do believe that they are invincible.

Today's businesses operate in a whirlwind of paradigm shifts – customers, markets, competition, technology – all change. There is the exponential growth of information – political and financial, hard and soft. Successful companies *must* be able to accommodate themselves and not simply try to force old patterns onto the new.

Out of Touch

So, one reason why companies fail to innovate is that they have become too stable. Their outlook, values, structure and so on are suited to a world that is no more. They are still providing for yesterday.

On the other hand, a company may fail to innovate successfully, because, although they are producing new ideas, these ideas are out of touch with the customer. Many a company is so protected from its customer that the only world it really appreciates is its own.

Hand in hand with being out of touch with the customer, a company may not innovate successfully because it makes assumptions about the world which turn out to be false. That is, as mentioned above, it may be stuck with a view of the world which is hugely out of date, or it may have a view of the present and future that doesn't correspond well with the world of today and tomorrow.

All of us have an intuitive sense of how the world operates and is developing. Some organisations, Shell for example, take the idea of trying to model the world and its markets very seriously. Forecasting is the name of the game. Such companies attempt to make their models of the world explicit, whereas for most of us they usually remain implicit. In making your model of the world explicit you can begin to analyse it and so, perhaps, improve its predictive qualities. This is the heart of the challenge. You may be able to predict the future accurately in the light of past and present trends in times of evolutionary or incremental change. The faster and more complex the rate of change, the harder this becomes.

In 1967, one American company, TRW, revealed the findings of a probe of future growth markets using the Delphic-oracle technique. It asked twenty-seven top company scientists to determine 'what the world would want and need in the next twenty years'.

Among the 401 emerging growth markets thus identified were a 500-kilowatt nuclear power plant on the moon, robot soldiers and germ-proof plastic houses. A year later, the National Institute of Dental Research reckoned that tooth decay and gum disease would be wiped out before 1980 by plastic teeth and tooth-decay vaccine. Not only was the technology to fulfil these dreams not ready, but forecasters did not bother to ask simple questions of the markets: e.g. would there really be enough customers for the predicted nuclear-powered underwater recreation centres . . . ?[4]

Mistaken growth-market forecasts[4]

Product	Year of forecast	Time horizon
Food into fuel	1961	unspecified
Jet-powered ships	1966	2 years+
Plastic housing	1967	13 years
Laser 3-D movies	1967	4 years
Hang-on-the-wall TV	1967	7 years
Family helicopters	1967	10 years
Undersea farming	1967	14 years
Fuel into food	1967	imminent growth
Home dry-cleaner	1967	5 years+
Tooth decay vaccine	1968	10 years
Foam-filled tyres	1968	unspecified
Roll-your-own cigarettes	1970	general trend
Steam car	1971	10 years
Plastic paper	1972	8 years
Moving pavements	1972	10 years

Of course, some of the growth-market forecasts turned out to be right but, all the same, out of the ninety forecasts studied for new products, new markets and emerging technologies more than half failed.

Checking Assumptions

So bearing in mind the old management joke that assumptions can make an 'ass' out of 'u' and 'me' (assume), what can you do to check the accuracy of your underlying assumptions? Three strategies come to mind. First of all, as stressed with the opinions you form of others, treat your view of the future or extrapolation as *tentative*. Type 2's always realise that extrapolation is a view, and never the truth.

Secondly, as with the judgements you form of others, try

to *disprove* your view. Prove yourself wrong. Challenge all underlying assumptions. Collect evidence that challenges or contradicts your view. This is, of course, difficult to do, because a forecast or model of the world is in itself a mind-set. Any mind-set encourages the holder to spot confirming evidence and discount or remain oblivious to disconfirming data. The third strategy helps overcome this.

This strategy involves generating *multiple views of the future*. Such a process should run in parallel with any strategic planning. Take a time-scale – 5, 10, 15, 20 years or even longer. Which time-scale you take depends upon the perceived rate of change and turmoil in your world. The greater the perceived rate, the shorter the time-scale. For that period of time generate six or more views of the future, each as different as possible and each containing centrally different and acknowledged assumptions. Beware of judging the probability of each future too early on: your existing model of the world with its often implicit assumptions will pervade and therefore misguide your judgement. *Consider each future as plausible.*

Figure 8.2   Multiple Futures

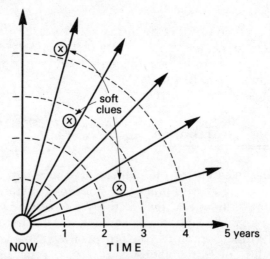

Having generated these multiple futures, you will become more sensitive to soft clues in the environment which previously may have been screened out or discounted. In other words the predicting of the futures is not primarily an attempt to work out which is the most likely of them. Rather it is a tool which helps you remain sensitive to a range of softer data that otherwise might be missed. Such insights can then be fed into your strategic thinking and plans for innovation.

An Impossible Science

In a sense, therefore, attempts to grapple with the 'world out there' can be seen as a form of scientific experiment. In such experiments you generate a hypothesis or hypotheses to explain what you think is happening in a given situation. You then test out these hypotheses by conducting critical experiments. If your hypothesis is disproved you look for a new one. If it is never proven, you *don't treat it as the truth* but as a working model of the situation. You and your colleagues continue to look for hypotheses that may account even better for what goes on in that situation.

However, in the case of business this is all a little trickier because you are not just trying to work out the what and the why of the present – but of the future too. Therefore you cannot carry out those critical experiments once and for all. You have to keep checking how well and badly each hypothesis or view of the present and the future is doing. You can then modify these existing views and generate new ones. Whenever you find that your view seems to be what is happening – beware. It's probably time to generate six or more new views!

Who Innovates?

The answer depends upon two related issues. The first, as already discussed, depends on how you decide to interpret the word 'innovate' – narrowly or broadly. The narrow interpretation implies 'Eureka Product Innovation' where you support a group of weird and wonderful specialists whose job it is to incubate and give birth to mind-shattering product possibilities. Such creative and crazed boffins may be difficult to integrate into the everyday organisation!

The broader interpretation of 'innovation' implies the generation of a whole range of implementable and profitable actions in pursuit of improving your process, procedures and products/services. This is 'Total Innovation'. By constantly pushing ahead on 'Total Innovation' you gain a multitude of competitive advantages.

The second issue concerns the extent to which you wish to have an entire organisation that is fit for 'Total Innovation' or, whether you prefer to have certain individuals or groups of individuals who are elected or self-selected to look after 'Total Innovation'.

The former route may require, especially in more mature industries, changing core values and restructuring your organisation. This will probably result in a much flatter and more 'fluid' organisational design. You are, in effect, saying that you have become too assimilative and now need to accommodate more. The old structures are not fitting the world. This approach may well take considerable time and effort. It will also require clever corporate architectural thinking and subsequent implementation. However, the total corporate mind will be more in tune with the world out there. And in time, as that world keeps changing, you will need to do it again and again. Ideally, you reach the position where there is constant change and evolution and not the occasional boot up the backside.

The approach of an 'innovative élite' (or subversion!) may be fine for 'Eureka Innovation' but in the case of attempts to stimulate 'Total Innovation' results in individuals working in a counter-cultural way – whether or not these individuals are self-styled innovators or set up by those 'on high' to 'change things round here'. In extreme cases, such individuals can be seen to be attempting to innovate *despite* the monumental stupidity and resistance of the organisation.

This 'despite the dinosaur' élitist approach is riddled with other problems too. First of all there is the problem of 'limited innovative focus'. 'Total Innovation' applies across an organisation. You may have launched one new product, which in itself may be a revolutionary innovation, and yet, simultaneously, have missed a hundred other opportunities for revolutionary and incremental product, service and procedural innovations. Elitist innovation will usually fail to see all these opportunities.

Secondly, by making 'Total Innovation' the concern of the few and not all, you encourage your people to focus too inwardly. Awareness of and sensitivity to your customers, whether actual or potential, is the prime ingredient for all successful innovation – if they don't want it, what's the point in the first place? Therefore to have specialist innovators only, can be to perpetuate too great a company-centric perspective. You miss out on many of the good ideas which can come from all individuals in an organisation, who all ideally have their eyes glued to the outside world. Furthermore, by not involving all your people in the question of 'What can we do that is better or new so as to increase our profitability?' you miss out on a key opportunity to increase people's sense of empowerment and belonging.

Thirdly, the specialist innovators have a massive uphill struggle. If the organisation's values remain 'old world', the very fact that the idea is new, creates enough of a problem in the first place. It is worse still, if the idea challenges existing power structures, functional boundaries, and even the existing business definition. To cap it all, if the innovation fails, the 'culprit' may be duly punished and thus demotivated from trying again.

This third reason explains, in part, the advent of the 'intrapreneur'[5] who is seen not simply as an ideas person but, primarily, as someone who has an excellent range of interpersonal and political skills. In stuck organisations, good ideas born of innovators may simply not survive. It seems a strange state of affairs that we have come to perceive organisations as being so resistant to the new that we have to introduce specialist individuals who have to find devious ways to circumvent the status quo.

If your innovative thinkers are too progressive, the culture of the organisation may simply, like the immune system in a body, reject the alien intervention. Your structure and values can become so rigid, that the organisation will be impervious to change.

In conclusion, to take the responsibility for 'Total Innovation' away from your people, is to set up your organisation as 'unaccommodating' and therefore ultimately as stupid. If you have a structure which encourages stupidity, people will often follow suit. And the last thing that (you or) your people are is stupid. Why make them so?

So the answer to the question 'Who is involved in the process of innovation?' – if we mean 'Total Innovation' – is everyone. But, you may say, we can't have people suddenly dropping their responsibilities to go off and try out some new idea! Therefore the question arises of how to organise for innovation.

A Model for Ideas into Action

It is probably helpful, in considering the question, 'How to organise for innovation?' to have some model or way of thinking about the *process* of coming up with ideas and turning these into profitable action. The model presented here has the acronym AGISA – which stands for:

–   Analysis,
–   Goal(s),
–   Ideas,
–   Selection,
–   Action.

1.   Analysis – identifying and pin-pointing those areas within which you wish to explore the possibility for 'Total Innovation'.
2.   Goals – following on from that analysis, setting the specific goals, be these problem- or opportunity-orientated, which you wish to explore.
3.   Ideas – generating all the possible ideas and solutions which could meet your goals.
4.   Selection – analysing, identifying and selecting those ideas which are most likely to achieve the goals.
5.   Action – the actual implementation process of translating those selected ideas into action.

This model is graphically represented in Figure 8.3.

Figure 8.3 AGISA

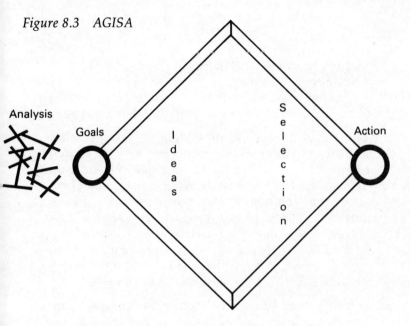

1. Analysis

The analysis stage aims to identify the key areas in which 'Total Innovation' is important. This exercise needs to be carried out regularly with, at least, your top teams – who are usually the guardians of the business definition, values and criteria by which all new ideas will be judged. It is therefore important that these top managers are aware of their own mind-sets, their hot planets, and the importance of creative listening.

Defining your business

Theodore Levitt, in his classic article 'Marketing Myopia'[6], has had a great impact on marketeers' and managers' thinking on how to begin defining 'what business you're in': 'The view that an industry is a customer-satisfying process, not a goods-producing process, is vital for all businessmen to understand.'[7] In other words, he argued, businesses too easily defined their activity in terms that suited their production bias, rather than in terms of what the customer wanted. For example, supposedly Hollywood ran into problems when TV began to take off because it defined itself as being in the 'movie' business and failed to see that it was in the 'entertainment' business. So, whereas your business definition may not affect your success in the short term, as markets and the environment change, your product myopia may leave you with no business at all!

> The classical example of this is the buggy whip industry. No amount of product improvement could stave off its death sentence. But had the industry defined itself as being in the transportation business rather than the buggy whip business, it might have survived. It would have done what survival always entails, that is, changing. Even if it had only defined its business as providing a stimulant or catalyst to an energy source, it might have survived by becoming a manufacturer of, say, fanbelts or air cleaners.[8]

So are you a 'railroad' or a 'transportation' company; an 'oil' or 'energy' company; a 'cosmetics' or 'beauty' company; a 'copy machine' or an 'office-productivity' company?[9]

Modern marketing gurus point out that you may reach a level of generality in your business definition that is so abstract it gives you every but no direction, or may set you up with too grandiose a view of yourself.[10] For example, if I am running a small taxi firm, it may be both helpful and yet dangerous to believe I am in the transportation business. It can be helpful in that I start to consider other forms of transport – motor bikes, bicycles; I may also begin to wonder what else I could transport – packages, animals, children. It might be unwise, however, for me to think of starting up a bus company! The challenging of your definition, can, providing it is done with sensitivity to the market-place, break mind-sets and keep you both customer and opportunity-focused.

New products and services

In the area of product or service innovation, a two-by-two grid can be of help (see Figure 8.4). Here you consider the four boxes of consolidation, expansion, breakthrough and revolution, by using the two axes of markets, existing and

Figure 8.4   Finding new products/services/markets[11]

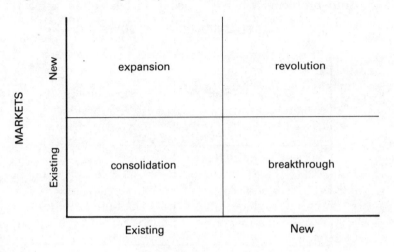

new, and resources, and products/services, also existing
and new. You then begin to consider how well you are
placed, both in terms of your market position and internal
resources, values and business definition, to consolidate
your existing position or move into one or more of the other
three boxes. You may see that you could well move into
a different box, but that this requires you to rethink your
business definition, values or structure. This then becomes
a question of return on investment, whether or not you
could afford the loss – (unless you are prepared to play the
eternal optimist's game of 'succeed or die') – and perceived
probability of success.

This is one area where your view of the 'world out there'
needs to be as free as possible of unacknowledged or faulty
assumptions.

Total innovation

A simple tool for identifying 'Total Innovation' issues is
another two-by-two grid (see Figure 8.5). This allows you
to focus on topics over and above product and service
innovation. To use this grid you need to generate a vision

Figure 8.5   Total Innovation grid

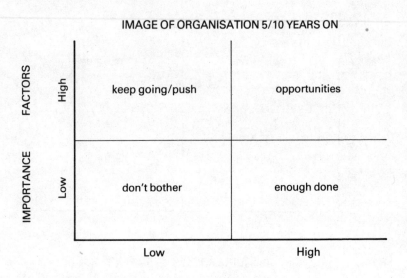

IMAGE OF ORGANISATION 5/10 YEARS ON

		Low	High
FACTORS	High	keep going/push	opportunities
IMPORTANCE	Low	don't bother	enough done

HOW WELL PERFORMING

for your organisation for a certain time in the future, say five, ten years or longer. The axes of the grid are the 'factors which you value as important' in ensuring you achieve that vision of the future and – 'how well you are performing on each of those factors'. This therefore gives you the boxes of 'don't bother', 'enough done', 'keep going/push' and 'opportunities'. Specific goals can then be drawn up for the 'opportunity' box and, to an extent, the 'keep going' box.[12]

As to the question of who is involved in this part of the process, the more people taking part in identifying and analysing areas for innovation and the subsequent setting of goals, the more they will buy into generating, selecting and implementing the chosen ideas. However, it may be inefficient to have all your people attending each and every strategy meeting! There has to be a balance between involvement and direction. If the top team or teams identify the general areas, these can then be passed on to individuals, functions and teams, according to relevance, who can then, in their turn, generate appropriate goals.

2. Goals

So, if we imagine that the areas for innovation have been analysed and identified by the top team or teams, these can then
be passed on to the relevant people. However, this stage is
as critical and important as that of Analysis. To understand
this it can help to see that a problem or opportunity can be
usefully analysed from several viewpoints:

Is the problem given or created?

On first hearing this may seem a very odd idea. A typical
response is 'We have enough problems as it is, without
trying to invent new ones!' However, this is perhaps the
most important of all areas to search as this is the domain
of opportunities. You can ask questions such as 'What can
we do differently, that no one to date has thought of doing?'
It also allows you to consider the seemingly impossible. For
example, many organisations consider growth of some five
to ten per cent to be difficult enough to achieve. Here
you can ask the question 'How can we make ourselves
twice/ten times as profitable?' In considering this seemingly impossible goal, completely new perspectives and
solutions may become available.

Is the problem fuzzy or defined?

'What is the square root of 278?' is a well-defined problem.
Most real-life and management problems are fuzzy. Such
problems as 'improving output, morale, market impact,
quality' and the like – are all fuzzy. That is, they are open
to being formulated or 'framed' in a myriad of ways. And
it was Einstein who said, 'The formulation of a problem
is often more essential than its solution.' For example, for
thousands of years, nomadic tribes appear to have accepted
the definition of a goal: 'To get the people to the water'.
This explains, in part, their roaming life-style. Seemingly,
one day, the goal became defined as 'To get the water to
the people'. Now whether the goal preceded the solution
of canals and the like is itself an interesting question – but
what is clear is that when you define a goal in a particular

way, your subsequent search for solutions becomes highly directed and therefore limited. On the other hand, if you gave your thinking no direction at all by having no goal at all, thinking at best would be inefficiently scattered and amount to no more than, perhaps, a fascinating day-dream.

So, you need to have specific goals but you also have to ensure that the goal is not encouraging a historical mind-set or stuckness. The Danish entrepreneur, Charles Kroyer, came up with the idea of a salvage principle for sunken boats which illustrates this point well. If he had simply stuck with the goal of 'to *lift* sunken ships', it would have greatly reduced the odds that he would come up with the idea of pumping polystyrene beads into the wreck, thus enabling it to 'float' up to the surface.[13]

A fun variation of this example of avoiding stuckness in the way that you frame a problem and the goal is the ping-pong ball problem.[14] You invite willing subjects into a room, pour them some coffee and then show them the problem. In the middle of the room you have set up a steel pipe that is fixed to the ground and at the bottom of the pipe there is a ping-pong ball. Their job is to get it out, without damaging it or the pipe and without removing the pipe from the floor. There are an assortment of objects lying nearby, such as a coat-hanger, a magnet, some string, a hammer and so on. You point out that they can use anything in the room to help them achieve this task. As you may have guessed, the problem is analogous to the 'floating' of wrecks, whereby the subjects can pour coffee down the pipe – or any other liquid which is to hand.

So, watch out for any stuckness, that may unnecessarily, be embedded within the goal itself. More of this in the next chapter.

Is the solution to your goal known or unknown?

This appears commonsensical. However, individuals in companies come up with goals which are then subjected to an array of creative problem-solving techniques – where the solution is already known by someone within or outside the company. For example, a group focusing on, say, a 'corporate communications problem' – their time and therefore money involved might be much better spent talking to consultants and other companies, who already have the answer – rather than reinventing the wheel and inappropriately using such creative problem-solving techniques.

3. Ideas

Having generated all relevant goals for innovation, you can apply the creative thought of the relevant individuals and teams. And in most cases, the range of goals will be so broad, that everyone can be involved in generating ideas on at least one or more of the goals.

Adaptors and innovators

Both in the identification of goals and the subsequent generation of ideas, some individuals will show a more revolutionary and others a more evolutionary approach. British psychologist Michael Kirton, has developed a robust and easy-to-use psychological instrument which establishes which of these two styles an individual prefers.[15] The 'adaptor' prefers to think within the existing structure and likes 'doing things better'. He or she will tend to be reliable, methodical, disciplined and efficient. Adaptors will prefer problems that come pre-packaged, already defined. They are usually sensitive to other people and therefore good in groups. They will rarely challenge the rules and norms of an organisation.

'Innovators', however, prefer to challenge the status quo and like to 'do things differently'. They enjoy breaking mind-sets and show little respect for tradition and custom. If problems arrive pre-packaged, they may question the definition given to the problem. They tend to challenge the rules, and may be less sensitive to others than adaptors would be. Innovators are usually the power behind the push for radical change – the problem is that they may want such change, even if it is not organisationally necessary! Whereas the innovator may want to trigger changes prematurely, the adaptor may wish to hang on to the status quo for too long. It may take a 'precipitating event' in the environment for adaptors to accept a change, which had been suggested by innovators some time earlier. In the same way that the mind maintains a balance between assimilation and accommodation, an organisation can be seen to achieve a balance between adaptors and innovators.

Understandably, extreme adaptors and innovators may not see eye to eye. At least, not until they understand that both styles of thinking have their advantages and disadvantages. In many, if not all cases, you need a blend of both.

Kirton makes some interesting observations about these two types. First of all the KAI (Kirton Adaptor/Innovator Inventory) does not attempt to establish how good a thinker or problem-solver you are. It is concerned with your style of thinking and not your level. That is, you find out the extent to which you prefer to think within the normal confines or 'frame' or how far you prefer to go outside that frame. It does *not* tell you *how good* you are at doing this, as this is a question of level and not one of style. Level is probably, in large part, determined by other factors such as that elusive characteristic, intelligence.

A second important point about adaptors and innovators is that, contrary to what you might think from the two labels, both types can be creative. Adaptors prefer to be creative within the frame and innovators outside it.

These two styles of thinking can therefore complement and, on the other hand, create friction. And the difference in the styles can appear right at the beginning of the AGISA process, as adaptors and innovators will tend to gravitate towards identifying issues that 'fit' their preferred 'frame-size'. Clearly this is not desirable as you want the innovation issues, resulting goals and ideas to be created, on the basis of what makes business sense and not what is simply comfortable to live with. For example, if an organisation is too innovative and is tending towards disorder, your issues, goals and ideas will need to be more adaptive. My experience with many organisations, however, is that the problem is more often than not the other way round. That is, you have a Board and company which have sat too comfortably for years in a fairly safe, uncompetitive environment, which now faces the need for revolutionary thinking and change. If their style is too adaptive they may fail to grasp the broader issues but, instead, will tinker with the existing array of smaller-sized problems.

This creates a fascinating dilemma. Some top teams are themselves exquisitely badly equipped to decide what innovative initiative is required. Furthermore, because they may prefer to think within the historical frame, they are oblivious to their now outdated assumptions about the world and market-place. Furthermore, they may be blind to those soft clues mentioned earlier on, which indicate that the world is not necessarily moving in the direction they thought and hoped.

Therefore top teams in particular, and most, if not all people, can take good advantage of knowing their Adaptor/Innovator score so that they can then caution themselves against unwarranted excesses in either direction.

Yes . . . but

'Yes . . . but' is often considered to be the arch-enemy of group creativity. True enough, a 'yes . . . but' may simply be picking up on the 5 per cent weakness in a proposed idea, which is otherwise very sound. And if the person doing the 'butting' is senior enough (entertaining enough!) or holds the floor for long enough whilst explaining the weakness of your idea, the baby may get thrown out with the bath water – the whole idea may well get lost. This destructive type of 'yes . . . but' goes hand in hand with critical listening. The mind habit of asking yourself 'What's good about it?'[16] when listening to the new is a helpful reminder that we are often too fast to flag an 'automatic no' when presented with a new idea. Such a habit also fosters creative listening.

Whenever you hear 'yes . . . but' in a conversation, prick up your ears. 'Yes . . . buts' can be very useful. Learn to spot and use them to understand what is happening between individuals and inside your organisation.

When you hear one person 'yes . . . but' the idea of another you may be witnessing a battle of frame-sizes going on between an adaptor and innovator. The innovator may want to reorganise the company to meet a new market need and the adaptor may simply want to send out a memo to advise suppliers of a new customer need – which in his view can be met through an existing product or service!

In this way the 'yes . . . but' alerts you that people have different views of what is happening and what is important. The soundest way to find out what is happening in the case of the market-place is to go and talk to your customers and find out what they want. And if you are still not sure, test out the two opposed and competing approaches/ideas on a small scale and see which best 'fits' the world out there.

There may be several other reasons for the 'yes . . . but'. Again, all of them give you useful information. These 'yes . . . buts' can be divided into 'Yes . . . but 1's' and 'Yes . . . but 2's'.[17]

To make this idea concrete, imagine a conversation where the marketing manager has just suggested the launch of a new service or product and has just received an overwhelming 'Yes . . . but'. In this sense the 'but' can take a variety of forms – from the folded arms of the listener through to the politer forms of 'That's very interesting. Mind you I'm not sure about doing it right now.'

So a 'Yes . . . but 1' can be born of a variety of reasons. These are:

- low ert,
- low level of imagination or relevant knowledge,
- high analytical competence with lack of complementary imaginative power,
- resistance to a person and/or idea that is perceived as threatening,
- one or both have different or wrong 'selection criteria' by which they are judging the idea in question, or lastly,
- the idea is terrible!

'Low ert' speaks for itself. Your idea just doesn't grab the interest of the listener. If this is a constant characteristic of the listener, he or she is probably in the wrong job (or is disaffected with life generally!).

'Low level of imagination or relevant knowledge' is also straightforward. Here the listener hears your idea and sees an array of problems with it. He or she does not have the requisite imagination or background knowledge to find a way forward so as to overcome the perceived problems. If such imagination and/or knowledge is critical for the successful performance of that job, develop the individual accordingly, or, if this does not suit the style or ert of that individual, move him or her to a better-fitting job.

'High analytical competence with lack of complementary imaginative power' – is probably the commonest of problems. For many people it is much easier to see what is wrong with an idea than to see how to improve it. It is also much safer to play at being critical. You never make any mistakes – and you don't achieve that much either!

This type of individual can, however, be nurtured into a great thinking ally. In the first place, it may be possible to encourage and develop within that person a complementary and more imaginative stance. With many people you only have to say a few times: 'That's a really sound objection. Now can you think of how we can get round it?' Or if you are happy with my jargon, 'That's a good "yes . . . but" *and* can you now give us the "and"?'

All the same some of these highly skilled analytical 'yes . . . butters' will not be able to equal on the imaginative front what they can achieve on the logical and critical front. Their left brain, that is, their analytical competence, is way ahead of their right brain, their creative and imaginative competence. However, don't brow-beat them into silence if they really find it difficult to 'and' their own 'buts'. In such a case, you can encourage the individual to become aware of the fact that he or she may tend to kill off ideas that could be nurtured into winners. Other people may often judge and feel that those who 'yes . . . but' a lot are negative and destructive. Therefore encourage your high-quality 'yes . . . butters' to state their 'buts' along with an invitation to 'and' – that is with an invitation to overcome their stated 'buts'. They can therefore say 'I like the sound of it but, as is usual in my case, I can see three problems. These are 1, 2 and 3. Have we, between us, got any ideas as to how we could overcome these hurdles?' Thus the highly analytical individual, who may wrongly be seen as an intellectual dinosaur, can be turned into a healthy catalyst for improving the quality of thinking and subsequent action.

'Resistance to a person and/or idea that is perceived as threatening' – either boils down to a straight interpersonal/

hot planet problem or a political one. If your organisation has some value around 'openness, honesty and integrity', the interpersonal/hot problem should not be too difficult, at least, to talk about. Shifting the owners of such hot viewpoints may, however, take some time. If on the other hand there is some politicking going on, this again is valuable information. For example, you may find that one function or department is resisting an idea, simply because it does not suit their personal interests. The function's priorities are out of line with the general strategy and/or values of the organisation. I, like most consultants, have witnessed this on numerous occasions where a part of the whole operates as though it were independent of the whole and resents 'interference' from 'head office', New York, London or whoever. Such 'segmentalism'[18] calls for a reinspection of values, structures and management style.

'One or both have different or wrong "selection criteria" by which they are judging the idea in question' – and this is perhaps the trickiest of all the 'yes . . . buts'. The trouble here is that those disagreeing will usually substantiate their position by arguing in favour of their point of view. 'What we should do is x, y and z,' says the one. 'Yes but,' comes the other, 'if we do that we will run into a, b and c. What we need to do is . . .' And on it goes. Both parties are making the mistake of leaving their implicit criteria, by which they are judging their own and the other's idea, unstated. The *implicit* needs to be made *explicit*. State what the criteria are that you are using to judge the suitability of the ideas under discussion. You can then move on to clarify or discuss the real heart of the problem. Your criteria often reflect a range of assumptions about the values of your organisation and how you see the business and market-place. Find out if your values are in conflict and address the issue directly. If your views about your business and the market-place diverge, again go and test your ideas. You can, thereby, update the assumptions that you hold about the world 'out there'.

So don't use your 'yes . . . buts' to convince others of the rightness of your point of view, but treat them as representing 'spokesmen for competing realities'[19] and then check which of those realities is fitting the world best of all.

'The idea is terrible' – speaks for itself. And yet, if people persist in coming up with ideas that get rejected, they are either ignorant of, or continue to challenge, the selection criteria that others accept. The greater the awareness of corporate values and the types of decision criteria that are best applied, throughout the organisation, the less this should be a problem. However, in the case of the individual who continues to generate seemingly daft ideas, and in so doing refuses to accept the shared decision criteria, you have someone who is either mad or a genius. He or she may be more in touch with the way the world is going than your organisation is. As you can rarely be sure which is which – there is a good argument that the top teams need to be aware of the murmurings of the supposedly crazy, as the crazy may have a much better view of the future than most! The Emperor has no clothes on . . .

'Yes . . . but, 2' or 'yes . . . but . . . and', appears on the face of it to be more constructive than the more often blocking and sometimes destructive 'yes . . . but, 1'. There are, however, both helpful and unhelpful 'yes . . . but . . . ands'.

The helpful ones are largely the reverse of the unhelpful ones. These are where the individual has 'high ert', 'high quality imaginative ability', and is 'open', in the sense of not being resistant to the new.

However, beware of a couple of 'yes . . . but . . . ands' that may lead you astray. The first of these is where you receive support and even euphoria for an idea, where that support is coming from individuals who are not being suffi-ciently analytical or thorough in their thinking, or who lack sufficient knowledge about the question in hand. Secondly beware of 'group think' where others are buying into your idea on the basis of agreement about underlying assumptions and shared criteria. These may be unacknowledged, go unchallenged and be ill-informed or wrong.

4.   Selection

Who decides which are the good ideas? Suggestion schemes have recently seen a revival in the UK – and these can be seen as an example of collecting ideas from the 'masses' – ideas that are then to be judged by others. And, in effect, most companies operate, at minimum, some informal suggestion scheme – 'If any of you have a good idea, let me know.'

The problem with this approach can be severalfold. These are:

– focus,
– criteria,
– rejection, and
– motivation.

The focus problem is that your people may come up with ideas that are not strongly related to business objectives, and instead focus more on working conditions. And although these ideas are useful, they are not adequately geared to the interests of the internal and external customer. And it is often the people 'lower down' in many organisations who have firsthand experience of customer behaviour and dissatisfaction.

Large and hierarchical organisations may also find that less senior people have a different or poor idea of the selection criteria which are used for deciding whether an idea is good or bad. And it may be that the decision criteria that more junior folk are using are *healthily* in competition with senior management. That is, the differing criteria may be giving you clear messages about a shift in values within the organisation or about a new view of what is happening to your customers and market-place. This challenging view often goes unacknowledged if there is no explicit discussion about decision criteria. Often, all that 'lowly folk' get to hear is that their idea has been rejected, or is being considered by the 'ideas committee' that doesn't meet again until late next month!

Thus you run into a motivation problem. How many times can you withstand the rejecting 'yes . . . but'? This is why some organisations have set up procedures whereby when an individual or function receives a new idea, they must reply within a limited time, say a week, and must first of all point out two things that are *good* about the idea. Doing this can, therefore, maintain the motivation of the creators of the idea and may also help the 'judge' of the new idea overcome such mind-sets as the 'NIH' – the 'Not Invented Here' knee-jerk response.

Ideally a response to an idea will not only be quick and constructive – it will also be used as an opportunity to state the selection criteria the judge is using. And this is so, if the idea is considered to be a winner or not. You may both agree that an idea is good, but have different reasons for considering it so.

In conclusion, the more you can encourage appropriate groups of people to focus on their innovation goals, generate and then select amongst their ideas, the greater the buy-in for subsequent implementation. Thus the question of Action and implementation – probably the most important and difficult stage.

5. Action

Here you come up against the central and interesting problem of the individual's 'zone of control' and 'zone of influence'. In simplest terms, your zone of control is your basic job – the things that you are expected, at minimum, to do. Your zone of influence describes everything else that you could possibly do so as to influence other people.

Older-world organisations prescribe the zone of control and make the zone of influence as limited or unrecognised as possible. Tight and rigid zones of control and attempts to limit zones of influence often reflect highly segmentalised and hierarchical organisations – 'You do this, my son, and only this. Do it well and you'll keep your nose clean.'

The problem is this. Organisations which are segmentalist, hierarchical and insistent on rigid zones of control and limited zones of influence may set up for innovative search only those issues which perpetuate the existing structure of the organisation. And it may well be that the existence of, say, two existing functions lies at the heart of a weakness to innovate in the customer's favour. For example, why should marketing, production and customer service/complaint functions be separate, watertight compartments in the first place? Surely the information your customer supplies, by way of a complaint, needs to be fed directly into the way you are making or marketing your product.

To illustrate the point, if you have briefed your customer complaint people to come up with ideas as to how to minimise customer dissatisfaction, they, in turn, may offer ingenious ways of offering fast compensation, replacement goods and the like. Could not the problem be addressed more fundamentally from the outset by including this 'dissatisfaction' function *within* production and marketing (and distribution, etc., all depending on where the sources of the problems are)? Any distance between your customer complaints and marketing functions is an indication of a dinosaur structure.

If you persist in an organisational structure which does not reflect the interest of your customers, you will have to rely on different functions' ability and desire to operate within their zones of influence, so as to bring about change in those other functions responsible for dissatisfaction. As with the general question of customer care, how far is your organisation designed so as to suit the precedent and convenience of yourselves, or designed to meet and maximise the satisfaction of your customers?

So assuming that you, as an organisation, are reasonably well structured for the interests of the customer, a range of teams can focus on different 'Total Innovation' issues. These, usually part-time teams, can be within a function or span across departments and functions. Teams operating within a single function may largely generate ideas which are within their zone of control so they can take responsibility through to actioning those ideas. If the ideas are, on the other hand, within their zone of influence they can pass them on to the relevant function. Teams which are cross-functional will be forced to operate more in their zone of influence.

The practical reader may be wondering what these ideas look like in action. The next chapter therefore focuses on some examples of attempts to stimulate innovation within various companies.

References

1. Drucker, P. F. *Innovation and Entrepreneurship*, Heinemann, 1985, p. 137.
2. Levitt, T. 'Creativity is not enough.' *Harvard Business Review*, 1963, Vol. 41, No. 3, p. 81.
3. See: Piaget, J. & Inhelder, B. *The Psychology of the Child*, Routledge & Kegan Paul, 1969.
4. 'Remember steam cars and plastic teeth?', *The Economist*, September 13, 1986, p. 71.
5. See: Pinchot III, G. *Intrapreneuring*, Harper & Row, 1985.
6. Levitt, T. 'Marketing myopia.' *Harvard Business Review*, July-August, 1960, pp. 45–56.
7. Levitt, T. 'Marketing myopia.' Ibid. p. 55.
8. Levitt, T. 'Marketing myopia.' Ibid. p. 52.
9. Kotler, P. *Marketing Management*, Prentice/Hall International, 1980, p. 67.
10. See: Kotler, P. Ibid. pp. 63–92.
11. Hodgson, D. 'Innovative Success in the Retail Financial Market', paper presented at the RBI International Retail Banking Conference, London, 1984, and see book of the same name, P A Consulting Services Ltd., Lafferty Publications Ltd., 1985.
12. This idea comes from within a problem solving software package, called 'The Innovator', produced by:
    Wilson Learning Corporation,
    6950 Washington Avenue South,
    Eden Prairie,
    MN 55344 USA
    or
    Wilson Learning Great Britain Ltd.
    23, London End,
    Beaconsfield,
    Bucks HP9 2NA
    England
13. Brown, M., & Rickards, T. 'How to create creativity.' *Management Today*, August, 1982, p. 38–41.
14. See: Adams, J. L. *Conceptual Blockbusting*, 2nd edition, W. W. Norton & Company, 1979, p. 54.

15.   There is an impressive amount of popular and academic material
       on Kirton's work. See, for example: Kirton, M. J. 'Adaptors
       and Innovators.' in *Innovation: A Cross-Disciplinary Perspective*.
       Gronhaug, H. & Kaufmann, G. (Eds.) Norwegian University
       Press, 1988.
       For information on the KAI, contact:
       Michael Kirton
       Occupational Research Centre,
       P. O. Box 109,
       College Lane,
       Hatfield,
       Herts AL10 9AB
       Tel. 07072 79781

16.   Sidney Shore's excellent bulletin, 'Creativity in Action' is the
       source of this positive mind-set. *Creativity in Action* is available
       from:
       P. O. Box 603,
       Sharon,
       Conn.
       06069 USA

17.   Many thanks to Tudor Rickards, with whom I originally hatched
       this idea.

18.   See: Kanter, R. M. *The Change Masters*, George Allen & Unwin,
       1984, pp. 28–35.

19.   I believe the playwright, Tom Stoppard, said this in a British
       television interview.

CHAPTER NINE

The Leading Edge

In the various attempts to tap and stimulate innovation in organisations, I have used the 'AGISA' model in one form or another. To make the model as understandable as possible, I have introduced various concrete ideas and techniques so as to communicate aspects of the model. As you read through this section you can work on a live problem or opportunity that you are currently concerned with.

Stage 1 – Analysis: 'Mind-Mapping'

Your Issue

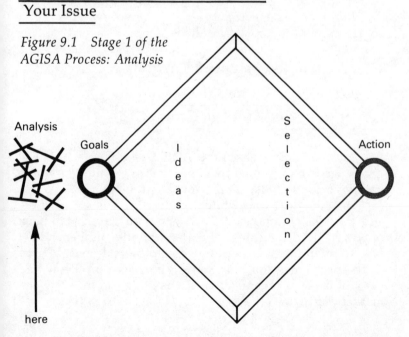

Figure 9.1   Stage 1 of the AGISA Process: Analysis

Analysis

Goals

Ideas

Selection

Action

here

More and more people are familiar with the technique of
'mind-mapping'.[1] Mind-maps allow you to pool all your
thoughts and ideas on a topic without constraint. In so
doing, you begin to see the connections and underlying
pattern of your thinking. Not only is the technique highly
effective, it is very easy to learn and apply in a range of
thinking tasks. To 'mind-map' a topic, start by jotting down
a keyword or phrase in the centre of the page. This is the
primary focus from which other thoughts, feelings, ideas
and images will spring. As these new ideas emerge, record
them, on one branch and then another. Any one branch
may divide or split into several sub-branches. In this way
you can begin to record the pattern within which your mind
holds and represents information. You will also begin to see
various interconnections between your ideas in the map. It
is often these links that are so important in understanding the
complexity of any issue. Such links may also be a source for
creative insight. You can represent these links, using arrows,
codes and colours.

Have a look through the sample mind-map in Figure
9.2. You can then map out your own chosen problem or
opportunity area (see Figure 9.3). In doing this *do not try to
define the problem/ opportunity* – just jot down everything that
comes to mind that relates to the issue.

Colouring in the Model of Thinking

Stage 2 – Goals: White and Grey –
Opportunity and Problem Goals

A colour code symbolises the AGISA (see Figure 9.4). The
goal stage is represented by white or grey. White represents
an 'opportunity goal' and grey a 'problem goal'. White
captures the idea of 'white light', which is everywhere
and yet usually unnoticed. The same, sadly, applies to most
opportunities. There are probably an infinite number and yet
it is so often much easier to focus on the bad news of grey
days – problems. You may solve a thousand problems and
yet still have an organisation that is failing to thrive in the
market-place.

Figure 9.2 Example Mind-Map

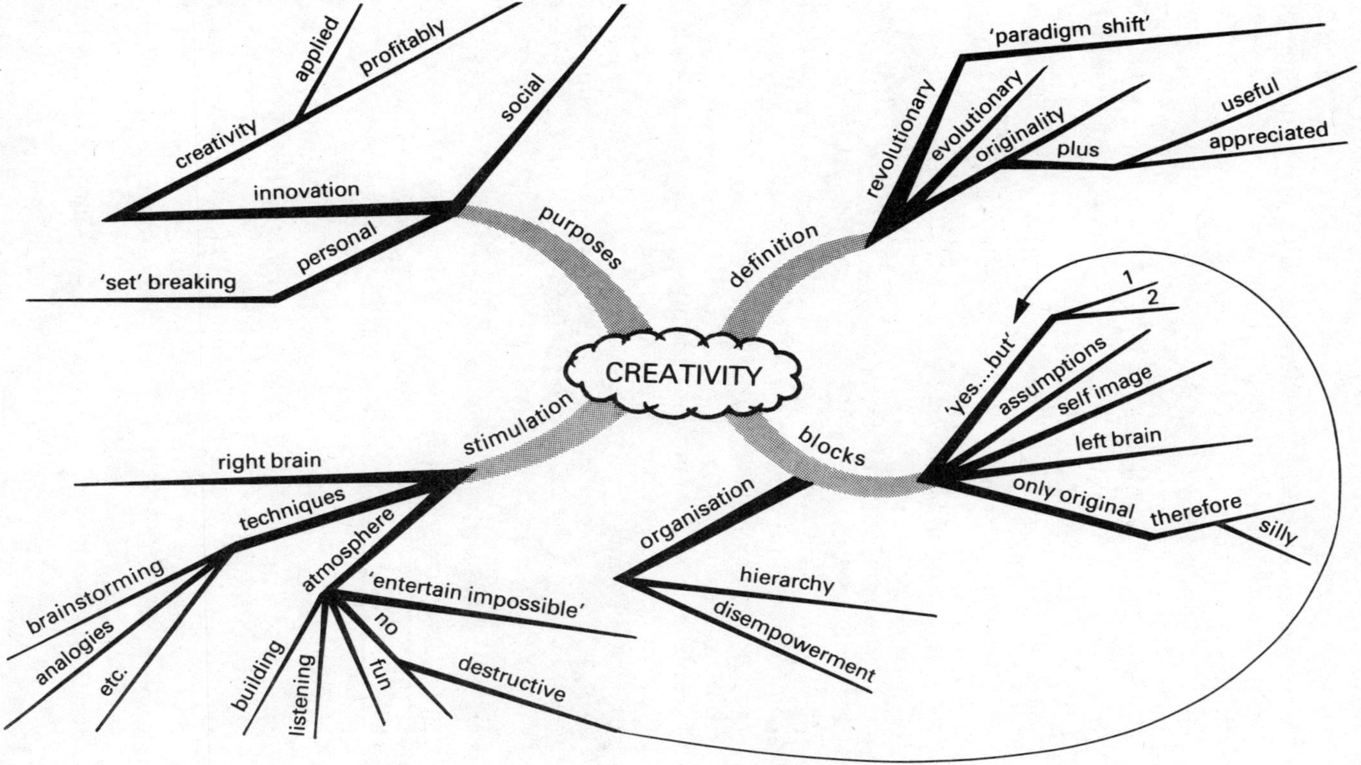

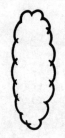

Figure 9.3   Mind-Map

Figure 9.4   Stage 2 of the AGISA Process: Goals

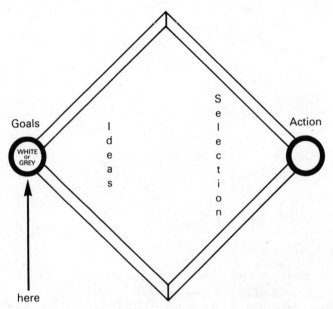

In looking back at your own mind-map, you may find that the original issue is looking even more complicated than before (a 'spaghetti' problem) or that the issue has split into several different issues (a 'blob of mercury' problem).

You may wish to check that you are neither thinking too narrowly or broadly about the issue. You may wish to set about consciously challenging your assumptions. 'What assumptions?' you ask. Only Type 1 thinkers never make assumptions! To get an idea of the ease with which we make assumptions, have a look at these two classic assumption problems.

The Nine Dot Problem

Here the task is to take pen or pencil and join up all nine dots/discs using four straight lines without taking your pen off the page or retracing a line. (See Figure 9.5.) Those who know this problem may like to try and solve it using just three straight lines. Then there is the one-line answer – where you join up all nine dots/discs using just one straight line. In fact, there are over six ways of solving the one-line version.[2] (See Figure 9.6 for solution.)

Figure 9.5   The Nine Dot Problem

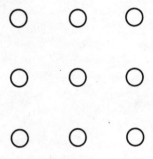

Don't worry if you didn't solve this – only a minority do. Some people in tackling it, however, show a clear tendency to stay within the apparent 'square' of the dots. If you break that assumption, you may then go on to solve it.

The Matchstick Problem

How can you construct four equilateral triangles out of six matches, where each side of each of the four triangles is equal in length to the length of one matchstick? You don't need to break the matchsticks! (See Figure 9.7 for solution.)

Many of us will have solved matchstick-type problems in the past. What is elegant about the solution to this problem is the way it highlights how we get stuck with the historical approach to the problem. We all know about three-sided pyramids and yet the mind-set is often too great to overcome.

This is why it can be a productive use of time to reflect on your mind-map, asking yourself the question: 'What assumptions am I making?' Having identified those assumptions, you can then begin to consider whether or not you feel it is reasonable to accept or challenge them. In doing this you may deepen your thinking about the issue in hand.

Now you can decide on the specific goal you want

to tackle. It is important that the goals generated are as productive as possible – that is they are not limiting the subsequent search for ideas and solutions. Avoid a 'multiple' or 'pre-emptive' goal. A 'multiple' could be: 'To improve morale and productivity'. Work on one specific goal at a time – in this case either 'morale' or 'productivity'. A 'pre-emptive' goal is one that has the solution already embedded within the goal itself, for example: 'To increase market share *by* launching new brochure'. The phrase '*by* launching new brochure' shows that the goal has already pre-empted the ideas stage and jumped straight through to the action stage. A goal needs to be stated so that you can then generate the widest range of ideas and solutions possible.

This simple but important point aside, there is then the more fundamental question of the level at which you 'frame' or 'formulate' your goal.

It may be helpful to think of the 'frame' for a problem as a 'calling pattern', where such a pattern contains the underlying structure of the problem or opportunity. For example, there is the old children's riddle (usually heard rather than seen in print), 'What is black and white and "red" all over?' As you probably know, the word 'red' should be written as 'read' (to rhyme with 'bed') in order for us to get the answer. The riddle acts as a calling pattern – that is, your mind attempts to meet the demands of the problem. You might, initially, come up with the solution of 'a badly wounded zebra', but this is not a very comfortable fit. 'A newspaper' is a better fit.

Not surprisingly, the higher up or more abstract the frame of your problem or calling pattern the wider will be your search for solutions (similar to the discussion on defining a business). This, in turn, creates variety and yet possible redundancy. The lower down or more concrete your problem frame, the narrower and often less original your solutions may well be. The exact key verb/noun in the problem frame also does much to limit and direct your search for solutions (remember the example of 'lift' or 'float' the sunken ship or ping-pong ball).

For example, let's take the serious example of the King's Cross Underground fire disaster, in London, 1987. Those involved in underground and subway safety might generate the high-level frame of: 'To enable people to "stop" any danger instantly' (note that the word 'stop' is quite broad a calling pattern keyword). A lower-level frame could be: 'To remove all the fire hazards from the London Underground'. Here, 'remove all fire hazards' is a fairly specific and limiting (although relevant) calling pattern. You would then come up with ideas like the removal of all inflammable materials and the like.

The high-level frame is creating a fair amount of potential redundancy for this specific problem because it ignores the need for escape from the tube. The lower frame may also be missing the point, at least from the angle of alternative forms of risk (bomb scare, toxic fumes, etc.). So although the two examples show a higher and lower calling pattern, neither necessarily fits that well.

Therefore a better higher-frame fit could be: 'To create freedom of movement for people/things from one space to another'. This frame is sufficiently high up or abstract

Figure 9.6   A solution to the Four-Line Version of the Nine Dot Problem

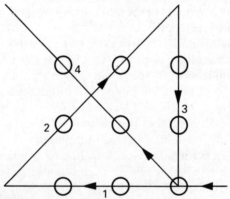

Figure 9.7   Solution to the Matchstick Problem

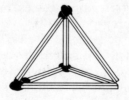

that you now have available a range of analogical situations for your search. Analogies are an especially rich source of information for creative insight.[3] When it comes to looking for ideas your thinking could range across such different areas as commercial exchange, industrial disposal techniques, distributions systems and so on.

A better lower frame could be: 'To enable people to leave an Underground complex safely'. However, although better fitting, the frame is narrow and may not help us think up some new solutions – that is, unless little thought has been given to this area before. And this is the important point about the frame-size – the more a problem or opportunity area has previously been examined, the higher the problem frame probably needs to be. Reframing is the natural tool of the Type 2 thinker.

Now how would you define your goal:

To_____

_____

Stage 3 – Ideas: Soft and Hard Blue

The ideas stage is represented as blue to capture the idea of breaking free of earthly constraints and encouraging 'blue sky thinking', or if you like, 'cloud cuckoo land'(see Figure 9.8). 'Soft blue' designates mildly original thinking, such as you achieve by using conventional thought-generating techniques, such as Help/Hinder from Force Field Analysis.[4] Inherent within this technique is the realisation that any system or organisation has forces attempting to push it in one direction, and at the same time, counter-forces pushing it in the other direction. As in an arm-wrestling fight, the one force may hold the other in check – that is, unless one arm is, or can be made, stronger and the other weaker. And this is exactly what Help/Hinder enables you to do in thinking about the forces working for and against the achievement of a goal. In this technique, having clearly established your goal, you think through and list (in the case of a team using a flip chart or overhead projector) all the ideas which will help achieve your goal. Then you list all the ideas hindering you. You then focus on what can be done to maximise the helping factors and minimise the hindering ones.

Figure 9.8   Stage 3 of the AGISA Process: Ideas

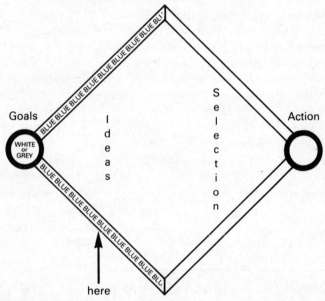

In a group context, this type of technique keeps members focused and stops individuals wandering off the subject and telling 'war stories'. In effect the technique helps people share and develop their more conventional patterns of thought. What is an existing idea for one person may be new for another. And through the process of one idea triggering another, the team may well generate some quite novel as well as useful ideas.

You can take your goal and work through those factors helping and hindering its attainment, listing these as illustrated in Figure 9.9, in the two central columns. You can then list those things which can be done to maximise the helping, and minimise the hindering factors. Wherever possible, see if you can push yourself to produce ideas that are *potentially practical* in the 'maximising' and 'minimising' columns – the extreme left and right columns. It is all too easy to jot down

Figure 9.9   Help/Hinder Grid

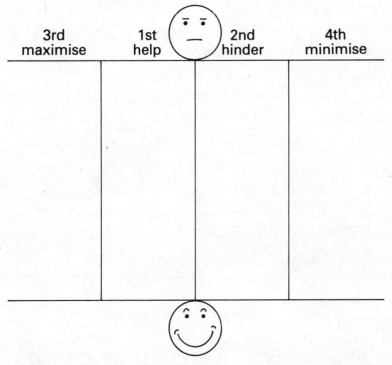

3rd maximise	1st help	2nd hinder	4th minimise

'noble intentions' – like 'try harder', but such woolly and vague ideas will probably simply be discarded when you reach the 'selection' stage of the AGISA process. Set your blue ideas up so that they are not savaged at the selection stage.

More often than not, it is 'hard blue' technique ideas which help stimulate more radical and original thinking. 'Hard blue' techniques challenge individuals to climb out of their conventional patterns of thought.

A good analogy is that of a sandy desert(see Figure 9.10).[5] If the sand slopes, imagine what happens as it starts to rain. Small channels are formed. As it continues to rain, the channels cut more deeply into the sand. The older the channel, the deeper it becomes. In this analogy, the channels or 'ruts' represent conventional patterns of thought. And very useful they are, at least, most of the time. But when we are looking for new ideas, we want to be able to get out of the channels; otherwise they have become habitual and ensnaring ruts.

Figure 9.10   The Desert Analogy

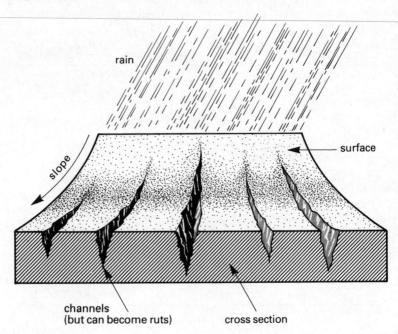

We are all used to the experience of having good ideas when we least expect them – driving, in the bath, relaxing, etc. What may be happening is that when your mind is no longer pondering a particular problem, you forget some of the constraints you had imposed upon your thinking. New perspectives or channels may thus be created.

'Hard blue' techniques help create these new channels – while remaining focused on the problem itself. Perhaps the best-known and yet most often misunderstood of 'hard blue' techniques is 'brainstorming'. There are, in fact, at least twenty-eight other idea-generating techniques, some more appropriate to some problems than others.[6] In essence, brainstorming and related techniques encourage you (or an innovation team) to 'entertain the impossible', to turn off the 'automatic no' response and so stop playing the game of being a premature and destructive 'yes . . . butting' 'idea assassin' (described to me some time ago as 'ideacide').

The techniques, therefore, aim to 'fool' the grid of experience – they drop you outside your normal channels of

thought. Hard blue knocks you 'rutless'. You then explore the
new terrain – that is, you entertain the impossible. Your goal
is to develop a new channel. Bear in mind, of course, that in
a team the ability to 'and' and 'build' on others' ideas is key.
Creative listening is essential.

Figure 9.11

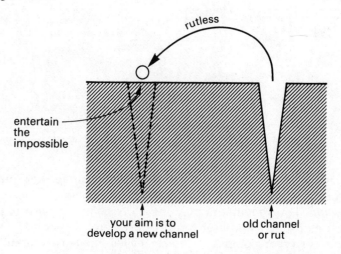

Hard blue techniques also aim to help you avoid falling
straight back into the rut you've just climbed out of – that
is, 'rerutting' as in Figure 9.12a. Some managers may find
themselves less than comfortable with such techniques and
experience the frustration of 'pogo' sticking up and down in
the same rut – Figure 9.12b![7] Type 1 thinkers will have very
great difficulty in 'entertaining the impossible' because the
starting-point for new thought will initially make *no sense*.
And you can guess what Type 1 thinkers will do with
'nonsense' – they will reject it out of hand, as in Figure 9.12c.

What happens when such 'hard blue' techniques succeed?
For example, imagine that you or a team are looking at the goal
of 'To improve customer care' (say within a bank). In brainstorming type techniques, 'crazy' solutions are welcomed as
starting-points for the thinking process. An individual might,
therefore, come up with the daft idea of 'All employees must
fall in love with every customer they meet'.

Figure 9.12

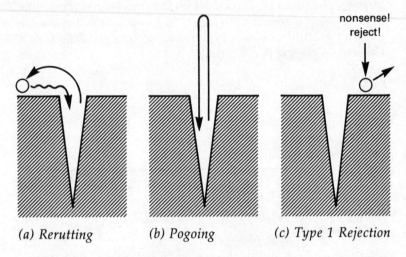

(a) Rerutting   (b) Pogoing   (c) Type 1 Rejection

This crazy starting-point is then 'entertained' *and* built upon, in an attempt to develop it into a *potentially practical solution*. Team members may therefore come up with ideas such as use of computer terminals, whereby personal data on a customer could be quickly called up (easily done if it is telephone contact) so that the conversation can be 'personalised', customer empathy increased, credit ratings achieved quickly and discreetly etc. Again, whereas, in some organisations, this may be an existing idea – that is within an existing channel of thought – here it may be genuinely new.

One reason why 'creativity' training and techniques established a bad name for themselves, is that the various types of trigger starting-point (random input[8] and analogies,[9] for example) are often not developed into concrete and potentially practical solutions.

This is a key point and can be well illustrated through the old game/exercise/test called the 'Alternate Uses Test'.[10] In this test you write down all the differing uses you can think of for an object, say a paper clip or a brick. The word 'use', as in 'uses of a brick' can be applied to mean 'as, for or in relationship to a brick'. This therefore widens the scope for original thought. The test is judged according to the number, variety and originality of uses generated. Try the exercise for yourself. Give yourself a minute to jot down all the different uses you can think of for a brick:

_____   _____

_____   _____

_____   _____

_____   _____

_____   _____

Adults typically come up with some five or six uses in a minute. And more often than not many of these uses are fairly conventional and not that thought-shattering. For example, many a manager will have jotted down, 'building with', and 'door wedge'. Fewer will have jotted down 'to stand on so as to make yourself three inches taller' or 'saving water by inserting a brick in a lavatory cistern'. So many of the uses are fairly predictable or 'reproductive' in the sense that they are easily available within the person's existing repertoire of thought. 'Productive' or more original ideas are rarer.

Life gets more exciting when you move on to the variation of the uses test, called the 'non-uses test'. Here, the game is the same, except, this time you are asked to jot down all the non-uses you can think of for a brick – that is, everything that you *cannot* use a brick *as, for* or *in relationship to*. Try this non-uses – again you have a minute:

_____   _____

_____   _____

_____   _____

_____   _____

_____   _____

Some find this 'non-uses' version easier than the 'uses' version – others not. The moment of truth comes when you ask someone to select his or her *best* 'non-use' for a brick – that is the thing or idea that could not be used 'as, for, or in relationship to' a brick. Select the best one from your own list. Now find a way, whereby the non-use can, in fact, be turned into a use! Possible contenders might be:

- to float,
- to think,
- to clean your teeth,
- and to create life.

Many a group delights in turning the non-use into a use. For 'float' they may say that it could be a wood brick or a brick that floats in mercury. As to 'think', you could contemplate or meditate on a brick – and anyway, in this game, we are thinking about bricks! 'To clean your teeth' might be challenged by the idea of using brick dust. And as for 'to create life' I recall one manager's idea of a short man and a tall woman! All these ideas are more original and some much funnier than the uses that come out of the conventional patterns of thought in the straightforward 'uses' test. You also find that people begin to challenge their assumptions about the word 'brick' itself – so a brick could be made of various substances, a 'fine upstanding fellow' can be defined as a 'brick' and so on.

A very useful point therefore comes out of the juxtaps-itioning of the 'uses' and the 'non-uses' test. In the uses test people come up with ideas that are conventional, sensible, serious, acceptable, existing – or in the left/right brain jargon (remember left-brain thinking tends towards more logical patterns, whereas the right tends towards 'softer', more original thought) – rather left-brain ideas. And, of course, if all our thinking is to follow conventional, sensible and acceptable patterns, we would never come up with one original thought. This point is essential to understand, otherwise all the creativity or 'imagineering' techniques look pretty daft. In a sense they are all daft – but *constructively* so. That is, they are designed to trigger unusual patterns of thought.

However, this important point is often lost on some more hard-nosed, perhaps more adaptive people, because, if the explanation stops here, there is a very real problem. Imagine if you asked the managing director or chief executive officer of one of the world's leading brick manufacturers to come and listen to some of the wild and wonderful new 'uses' we have found for bricks – to float, to ponder upon, to grind down and turn into an abrasive for cleaning your teeth, for facilitating vertical sexual intercourse, and the like. He or she would quite rightly think we had completely lost our marbles!

There is a very real difference between the randomising of thought so as to come up with an *original* or novel thought and the translation of the original thought into a *creative* thought. If 'originality' is represented by the letter 'O', creativity equals 'O' *plus*. And *plus* here means that the idea must be appreciated – i.e. in business make money, or in medicine save lives. In art the question of the *plus* is sometimes harder to fathom. Some people did not judge the exhibit, made of bricks, in the Tate Gallery in London, as creative. In business, however, the *plus* is usually easier to see. And few people, indeed, would see our brick ideas as being 'O' *plus*.

Therefore a creativity technique can help trigger some original ideas – these have then to be beefed up and transformed into potentially practical solutions.

For an example, outlined in Figure 9.13 is a creativity technique I have recently developed (and as with most ideas it is based upon a combination of existing techniques) called 'Framing Up and Down'. Imagine that I am working on the goal of: 'To increase the sale of "wall coverings" – i.e. paint, wallpaper and related products'. And assume that I have decided to focus on 'paint' as the starting-point.

You can then apply the idea of 'reframing' and in this case the special ideas of 'framing up' and 'framing down'. An example of a reframe is to see 'paint' as a 'wall covering'.

A 'frame up' would be 'liquid' and a 'frame down' – 'pigment'. In other words, a frame up (U) is a frame that is larger than and yet also includes the lower frame along with many others. A 'frame down' (D) is a frame that takes only an aspect or gives an example of the higher frame.

Lastly you have the ideas of a 'hard' (H) and 'possible' (P) application. All the final hard applications can then be

Figure 9.13 Example of Framing Up and Down

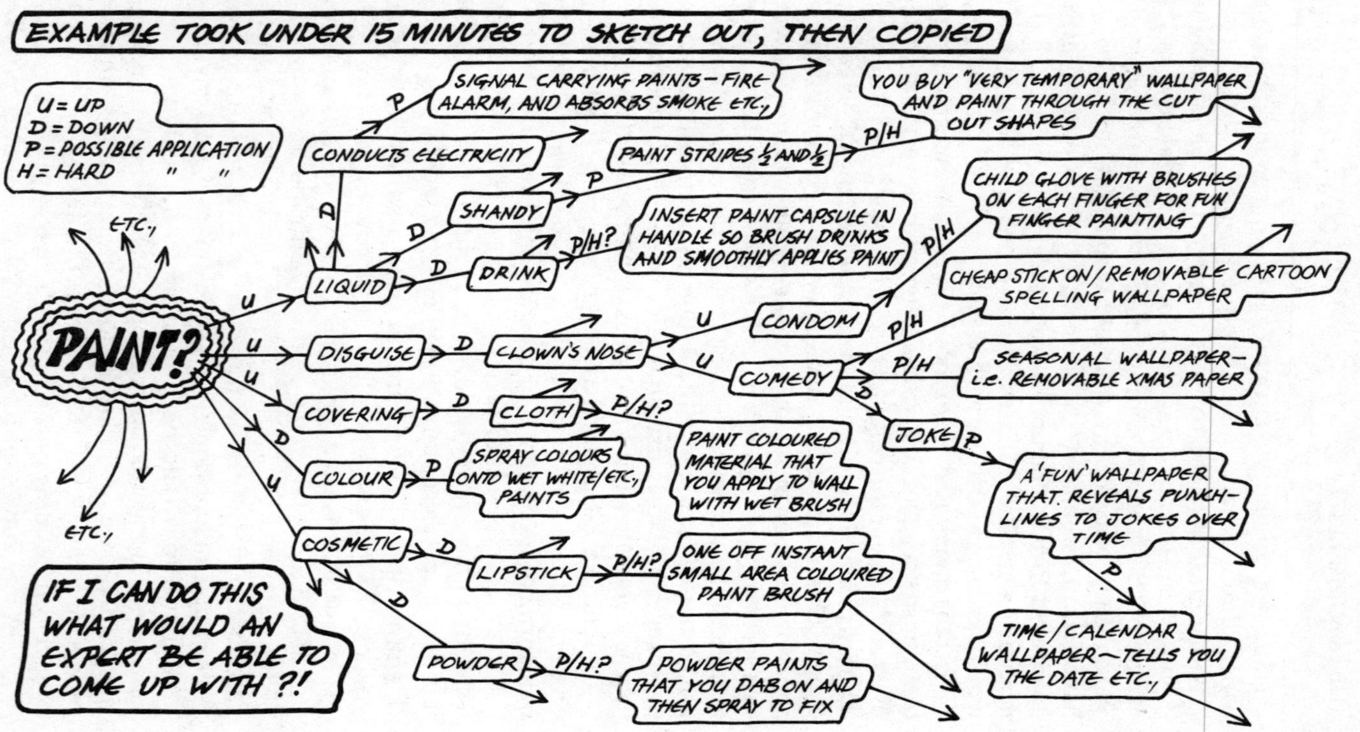
EXAMPLE TOOK UNDER 15 MINUTES TO SKETCH OUT, THEN COPIED
U = UP
D = DOWN
P = POSSIBLE APPLICATION
H = HARD " "
PAINT?
ETC.,
ETC.,
U
LIQUID
D
CONDUCTS ELECTRICITY
P
SIGNAL CARRYING PAINTS – FIRE ALARM, AND ABSORBS SMOKE ETC.,
D
SHANDY
P
PAINT STRIPES ½ AND ½
P/H
YOU BUY "VERY TEMPORARY" WALLPAPER AND PAINT THROUGH THE CUT OUT SHAPES
D
DRINK
P/H?
INSERT PAINT CAPSULE IN HANDLE SO BRUSH DRINKS AND SMOOTHLY APPLIES PAINT
U
DISGUISE
D
CLOWN'S NOSE
U
CONDOM
P/H
CHILD GLOVE WITH BRUSHES ON EACH FINGER FOR FUN FINGER PAINTING
U
COMEDY
P/H
CHEAP STICK ON/REMOVABLE CARTOON SPELLING WALLPAPER
P/H
SEASONAL WALLPAPER – i.e. REMOVABLE XMAS PAPER
D
JOKE
P
A 'FUN' WALLPAPER THAT REVEALS PUNCH-LINES TO JOKES OVER TIME
D
TIME/CALENDAR WALLPAPER – TELLS YOU THE DATE ETC.,
U
COVERING
D
CLOTH
P/H?
PAINT COLOURED MATERIAL THAT YOU APPLY TO WALL WITH WET BRUSH
D
COLOUR
P
SPRAY COLOURS ONTO WET WHITE/ETC., PAINTS
U
COSMETIC
D
LIPSTICK
P/H?
ONE OFF INSTANT SMALL AREA COLOURED PAINT BRUSH
D
POWDER
P/H?
POWDER PAINTS THAT YOU DAB ON AND THEN SPRAY TO FIX
IF I CAN DO THIS WHAT WOULD AN EXPERT BE ABLE TO COME UP WITH ?!

considered at the selection stage of the AGISA process, where they can be judged against such criteria as feasibility, technological fit and so on.

What this example shows is that it is the translation of the unusual starting-points which is the key to the success of creativity techniques. You are, in effect, always asking yourself the question 'How can I use this apparently daft starting-point to come up with a potentially practical solution to the goal in hand?' That question 'How?' seems to be key.

You can now take your own goal, and having tried the 'soft blue' technique of Help/Hinder based on Force Field Analysis, try a 'hard blue technique'. If your goal is to do with product or service development you can try Framing Up and Down. For any other issue you can try a variation of a brainstorming technique, called 'Get Fired'.[11] Here, bearing in mind your goal, jot down five solutions/answers which are so crazy that your work colleagues would be seriously concerned about you if you started coming up with this quality of ideas at a normal meeting. Make sure the five are so crazy that even you blush! Completely forget about the 'real' world!

Five Crazy Solutions

1 _____

2 _____

3 _____

4 _____

5 _____

Now select the three craziest – the ones most removed from common sense (once defined to me as 'stupidity hardened by habit'!).

Take the first of your three craziest ideas and *entertain the impossible*. Consider how you can use this daft starting-point

as a trigger to develop *potentially practical solutions*. Don't
worry if the crazy starting-point initially suggests another
equally daft or even dafter idea. Jot all these ideas down. Use
the question 'How?' to challenge each one of these bizarre
ideas along the lines of: *'How can I use the idea of'* – 'train all
our people to become telepathic' ('Get Fired' idea) to achieve
the goal 'To improve internal communications'? You never
have to take the crazy idea *literally*. It is simply suggestive of
various starting-points/ideas. You may then come up with:

–   graffiti boards,
–   special half-hour insight presentations into individual's
     jobs and feelings about the organisation,
–   electronic mail, photos and names of all people on
     notice boards,
–   kidnap/swap a member of your team for a member of
     another team – job rotation, weekly rotation, etc.

Some of these ideas may be within your grid of experience
and others new. The emphasis is on using the daft idea to
generate ideas sufficiently practical to carry, along with the
solutions from Help/Hinder, to the next stage, selection.
    Have a go.

YOUR GOAL

To ....

....

Crazy idea 1:

_____

_____

Ideas that come to mind:

_____

_____

_____

_____

_____

_____

_____

Crazy idea 2:

_____

_____

Ideas that come to mind:

_____

_____

_____

_____

_____

_____

_____

Crazy idea 3:

_____

_____

Ideas that come to mind:

_____

_____

_____

_____

_____

_____

So white is for opportunity, grey for a problem. Soft blue describes mild creative thought and hard blue more extreme creative thought. And in the blue phase you are aiming to generate ideas that are original *and* potentially practical. However, they do not have to be fully working and acceptable solutions.

Stage 4 – Selection: Red

The selection stage is the time to select, fine-tune your ideas and solutions, or if they simply cannot be improved adequately, they have to be discarded. The selection stage is red, as this is the time for saying 'stop', as at traffic lights, and thoroughly analysing the idea (see Figure 9.14).

Whereas during the 'blue'/ideas stage 'yes . . . but' is completely discouraged, here, at the red/selection stage, 'yes . . . but . . . *ands*' are encouraged. That is, although this is the time for seeing what is the matter with an idea, both you individually and teams generally are to be encouraged to go red/blue. You highlight what is the matter with an idea and then see whether you can develop it, using creative thought, so that it overcomes the identified weakness.

Figure 9.14   Stage 4 of the AGISA Process: Selection

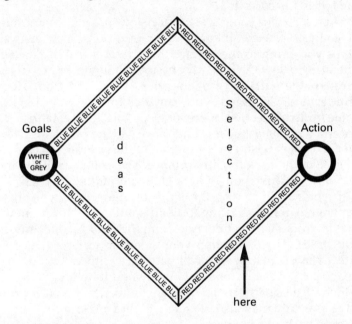

Much of the time it is obvious which idea/s you want to carry forward for actioning. Selection is often an intuitive or right-brain process. Human beings excel at this type of 'soft' decision-making. You can often bring years of experience to an issue and instantly know the way ahead or the decision to make. However, the problem with intuition, as with your judgements about other people, is that it can be right off the mark. Intuition can be good and bad. The difficulty is knowing which. For example, I recall being asked to think through this problem:

Imagine a paper tissue that is 0.001 inch thick. Now fold that tissue in half. Again, fold it in half. And although it is practically impossible to do it, imagine that you continue to fold the tissue in half for a total of fifty times. How thick will the folded tissue have become?

My intuitive mind sensed it would be quite thick or tall – perhaps a few hundred feet high. My analytical mind kicked in to remind me of the multiplying effect of compound interest and the like. So, I guessed – 1,000 feet high.

The answer – some 17,770,000 miles tall! I sat there amazed and disbelieving. But my left brain and my calculator tell me the answer is correct.

Therefore, in complicated decision-making some form of analysis can complement your intuition. Such analysis helps you bring to the surface those factors that are usually operating below the level of conscious thought. To help think through the suitability of the ideas generated from Help/ Hinder and Get Fired, you can therefore usefully employ some form of selection matrix or grid. This helps establish the criteria which *must* be met and those which you *want* to have met. You may wish to weight each of the criteria – to capture a sense of their relative importance. The examples in Figures 9.15 and 9.16 give you an idea of how grids can be used.

If you want to try the grid on the ideas you have generated, first of all bring forward your ideas (old and new – that is, from Help/Hinder and from the hard blue technique you used). Then establish your selection criteria (i.e. cost, effectiveness, manpower, compatibility with your company image etc.). As mentioned, you may find it helpful to decide which of these criteria *must* be met and which you *want* to have met. You may also wish to weight your criteria – either scoring each out of 10, where 1 means not important at all, through to 10, meaning – absolutely must be met; or you can share out a fixed number of points – 10, 50 or 100, for example, whereby the more important your criterion, the more points you allot to it.

List your various blue ideas down the left-hand column of the matrix, with the criteria along the top. Decide whether or not to score each idea against each criterion (i.e. 0 = doing very badly, 10 = doing very well) or simply say 'yes' or 'no'. If you do decide to use the weighted criteria and, in turn are scoring each of the ideas out of ten, you will then need to multiply the weighting of the criterion by the score you have given that particular idea.

What has been described so far, however, is really the 'old world' use of grids. To bring some creativity/blue into the process, what is probably most effective is to circle all the 'no's', or if you have used a scoring out of 10 system, circle all scores below 6. Then to turn this old-world technique into a new-world one, try to turn all the 'no's'/low scores into 'yes's'/high scores. That is, it is now time to 'Yes . . . but . . . and'. And in the light of your 'Yes . . . but . . . ands' you will be able to modify the ideas listed in the left-hand column. If, however, you cannot modify the idea, and you decide that it is failing on a critical *must* criterion, you will obviously need to strike it off the list of ideas/solutions. The overall intention of the grid is, however, to select all the sound ideas, and as far as possible, to help an idea that is 'limping' to be transformed into a real winner.

In practice it may be useful to encourage yourself and teams to think through the decision or selection criteria *before* they go into the blue techniques. Although, theoretically, you might argue that to establish the criteria before thinking of the ideas, would be to limit the scope of those ideas, what usually happens through establishing the criteria first of all, is that the quality of thinking is improved.[12]

Stage 5 – Action: Green

So, if the aim of the game is 'ideas into action', you have the final stage of 'action' and this is captured by the colour green. Green, again as at traffic lights, is for *Go* (see Figure 9.17).

At this stage you need to think through at least some of the following questions – and you can fill in your thoughts for the real ideas you have selected:
Who do you need to persuade?

Figure 9.15   Simple Selection Grid

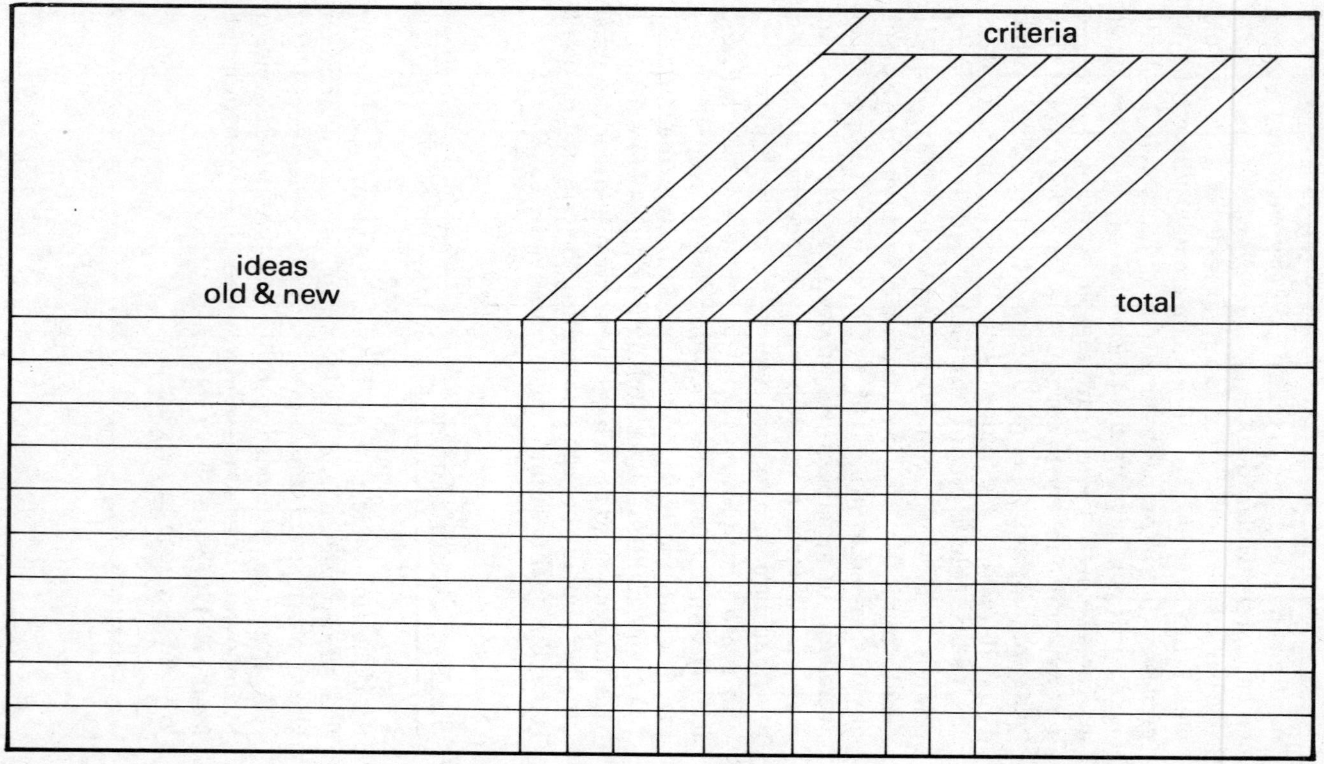

Figure 5.16   Weighted Selection Grid

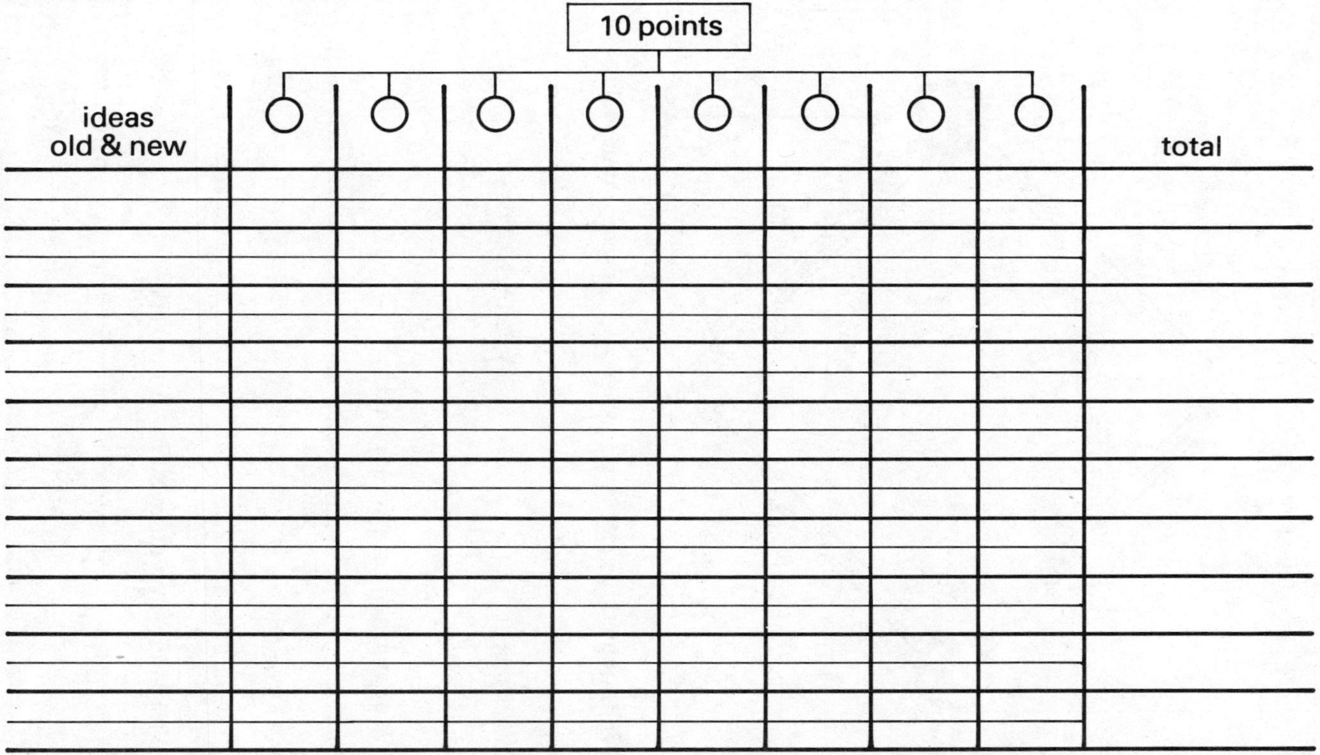

10 points

ideas
old & new

total

1. Establish weighted criteria.   2. Judge ideas out of 10.   3. Multiply 1 by 2.

Figure 9.17   Stage 5 of the AGISA Process: Action

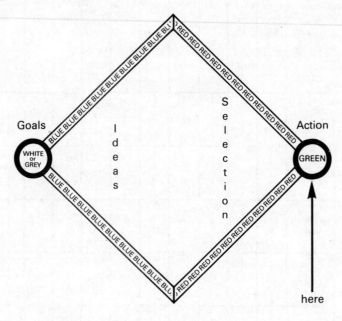

What objections can you foresee and therefore remove?

_____

What research do you need to do before starting?

_____

What are the timings involved?

_____

What are the costings?

_____

Whose 'ert' do you need to win over?

_____

Where are you going to do this?

_____

What equipment will you need?

_____

Exactly what are you going to do, by when?

_____

How can you monitor and measure your progress?

_____

In other words, in most organisations, the first four stages of the AGISA process are together easier than this last stage on its own. 1 per cent *inspiration* and now for the 99 per cent *perspiration*. Those who have made a healthy habit of innovating probably apply as much of their creativity to thinking through the barriers to implementation, as they do to generating the ideas in the first place.

Don't Collapse the Model

Once you begin to think through the model, you realise that there may be an understandable degree of tension between the different colours. Whereas the 'blue'/ideas stage is wanting to diverge and open up issues and ideas, the 'red'/ selection stage wants ideas to close down: convergence is the goal here. In the meantime, the 'green'/action phase is waiting impatiently for the thinking stages to be finished.

In the same way that certain individuals prefer a more adaptive or innovative style of thinking, individuals will also show themselves to be more comfortable and perhaps more competent at different stages. For example, a very 'blue' thinker may excel at the ideas stage, whilst his or her more 'red' colleagues may look and listen on aghast.

In a nutshell, blues may see reds as blocking, critical, 'yes
. . . butting', and unimaginative; on the positive side the
blues may recognise that reds stop them pursuing half-baked
ideas by introducing hard-nosed realism.

Reds will often see blues as crazy, unrealistic and wacky;
on the positive front, their redeeming features may be seen
as offering the unusual insight, starting off a new train of
thought and challenging unwarranted assumptions.

Lastly, how will the blues and reds see the greens – those
whose natural preference is for doing things, for getting on?
Greens are often seen as achievers, who are impatient, who
perhaps even love fire-fighting to the extent of going around
and lighting their own to keep themselves busy! If the
criticism of greens is that they may act without sufficient
thought, their great strength is that they do at least get things
done – even if they may be the wrong things!

Greens, in their turn, may see blues and reds as wasting
time. Greens often see meetings and discussions as unnec-
essary and time-consuming. However, the green individual
may recognise that the blues and the reds do, at least some
of the time, produce, between them, high-quality ideas.

Clearly, it is too simple to stereotype thinking into such
simple and distinct categories. In the same way that you
cannot pigeon-hole people, any one individual may show
the ability to move through all the colours. All the same, you
may show a stronger preference towards one colour than
another. The idea of the colours is to sensitise people to the
different stages of the thinking process, so that each stage is
fully explored and not interfered with by prematurely moving
on to the next stage.

However, you often find that stages are missed out or one
is collapsed into another.

Beware therefore:

*Figure 9.18   The company which recognises problems but then
fails to tackle them, or which only focuses on problems and never
or rarely opportunities.*

Figure 9.19 Crazy implementation – the company which misses out on the red stage. All ideas get implemented.

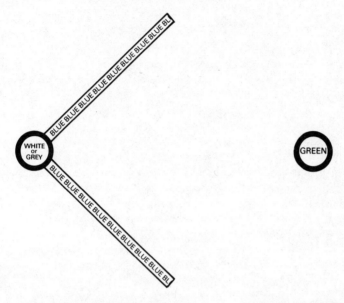

Figure 9.20 Transcendental hesitation[13], where there is a failure to open up thinking adequately at the blue stage, so that all the options that are generated are mediocre and rather similar – as a result you spend ages trying to decide between very unexciting alternatives!

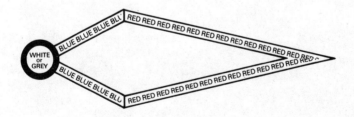

Figure 9.21 Frustration where the reds start closing down while the blues are still trying to open up.

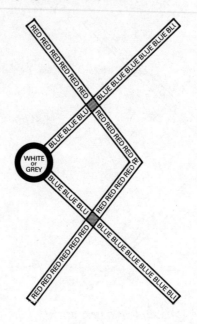

Figure 9.22 Too busy to think!

Figure 9.23 Great expectations but nothing finally implemented.

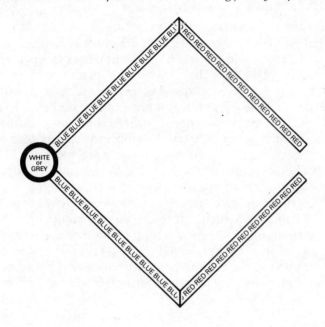

AGISA in Action

Finally, let's look at some specific attempts to stimulate innovation.

The Inspired Trainer

Many a time I have been asked to run seminars on creativity, innovation, breaking mind-set, creative problem-solving – where that request has come from the 'training' function. Often, this creative initiative goes counter to the culture of the organisation. The trainer has decided the company needs creativity. Sadly, as already discussed, many training functions have low credibility.

These seminars, in banking, in the oil industry, for computer companies, etc., are usually very well received. *But* at the end of most, if not all, comes the inevitable *but*

– 'My boss doesn't want me to be innovative' – or 'My boss wants me to innovate, but I don't feel that the culture overall wishes me to.' The organisation has neither recognised the general need for stimulating Total Innovation, nor has it, therefore, attempted to identify relevant issues for such Total Innovation. Although there may be a place for creativity training for specific groups, i.e. marketing and R and D (research and development), there is little point in trying to stimulate creativity generally through the odd course or seminar. Such seminars may develop individuals, but will simply create confusion and friction in a work context.

I recall one general manager of a large assurance company telling me that creativity was something he wanted to *reduce* amongst his sales force! There was also a request from one UK tobacco company which wanted creativity training for their middle and junior managers. I pointed out that this initiative ran quite counter to the hierarchical and fairly rigid structure of the company. To try and stimulate creativity would be to set those managers up to fail or become frustrated or both.

Brian – Creativity Software

So, hitting the middle belly of the organisation with training which is out of line with what the head wants will have little if any effect. It may have simply been an organisational irritant.

However, you occasionally find a manager who has a department or function where the style and values are largely set by that person. In one large financial institution, one such manager decided to run a series of creativity seminars with the clear intention that the new learning be transferred back to the work-place. The total organisation, in my opinion, is and was unreceptive to the idea of creativity; at best it is a dynamic dinosaur. This move was therefore very counter-culture.

Following the creativity seminar this manager's team developed their own special 'time-manager' sheets which simulated the creative problem-solving process of AGISA. In the following year we co-developed a creativity software package, containing the AGISA process and also including a decision-making routine, an opportunity-finding process (new markets, new products and services) and lastly a planning routine that helped think through all the barriers to implementation of ideas. 'Brian', as it was called (it was to be called 'Brain' but we thought this too arrogant) also introduced the new user to the Learning Style Inventory of American psychologist, David Kolb,[14] which is designed to establish your preferred style of learning (not dissimilar to the blue, red and green colour concept). In the planned final form 'Brian' was meant to switch its style according to your score on the LSI. Sadly the manager responsible left before we were able to do this. He left, in good part, because he was leading a small-scale counter-cultural movement and his bosses didn't like it!

Leading Edge Teams

A 'Leading Edge Team' is usually a *part-time* team which has been skilled in a range of creative problem-solving techniques – and works well as a team. In the same way that the individuals begin to realise that different styles of thinking complement each other in the thinking process, they can come to appreciate that different styles of personality can complement each other in teams. The work of Meredith Belbin, on the different types of team member, can be a valuable insight to any group you wish to help turn into a synergistic team.[15]

I have been involved in setting up and training over a hundred such teams. Some have worked on short-term projects and others run on. Some have faltered and others have thrived.

A faltering example comes from the heavy engineering industry. Here we trained cross-functional and multi-level teams to tackle seemingly intractable problems. There appeared to be Board support. The teams were, in effect, freelance problem-solvers, and if your function had a tough problem, it could pass that problem/opportunity over to a Leading Edge Team to see what they could come up with.

There emerged two problems. The teams were not actually implementing their ideas, they were simply making recommendations. Secondly and most importantly the teams represented a set of values which were not that well reflected in the rest of the organisation, nor across the Board. These teams, in my opinion, limped.

So, from the faltering to the successful. A substantial British leisure company, for some time, had run an initiative to try and 'enhance the service' provided to clients. This was a natural part of the company's overall concern for increasing competitive advantage.

However, this initiative had run into difficulties. People in the organisation did not necessarily know exactly what they were meant to be focusing on in pursuit of 'enhancing the service'. And the initiative had become associated with even more paperwork. The objective was also seen as emanating from head office – and there was more than a touch of 'them' and 'us' in the first place.

We discussed how we could set up a completely new initiative which would inspire everyone to come up with new ideas to enhance the quality of service – and in turn translate these ideas into action.

Initial meetings were held with all the managers, usually lasting two days, where we discussed why it was important, in competitive terms, that we continue to come up with ideas for service and quality that outstripped the competitors. We discussed how to set up 'Leading Edge' so that the ideas were generated and implemented and did not simply get referred up or across. We did not want to run the risk of flooding the organisation with thousands of unimplemented ideas. Simultaneously, during these meetings we turned the negative stigma around the previous initiative to a positive feel for this new one – simply through explaining the importance of Leading Edge and involving them in the design process.

I had some sense of how this Leading Edge initiative and the teams would be set up before these meetings/ briefings started. However I worked very hard not to impose these ideas onto the managers. Instead I wanted their full commitment and enthusiasm. This was finally achieved.

By the end of the first round of seminars, the managers had decided on the acronym of PISCES, which stands for Profit, Image, Service, Care, Excellence and Savings. The teams to be set up therefore had and have this general banner within which they could and can generate their own goals. If you like, the top teams had defined the scope for 'Total Innovation' – PISCES.

A team of internal trainers were then trained so as to be able to set up and train Leading Edge Teams. Within that training there was the theme of 'empowering'. That is, the sense that the 'organisation is the people' was stressed – and people bring about change. More of this in the next chapter. However, so as to curtail the tendency that teams might just come up with ideas which were for everybody else to do, and none they could actually do anything about directly themselves – for example ideas like, 'reorganise the company', we suggested the '90/10 per cent formula'. This simply means that the teams are encouraged to come up with ideas that are 90 per cent of the time within their zone of control and only 10 per cent within their zone of influence. This formula helps teams focus on what they can do – *now* – so as to make a difference. Ideas that they do have about other parts of the organisation are, of course, never blocked.

If a team feels that an idea they have communicated (and therefore, by definition, one that is only within their zone of influence) is being blocked, there is a 'court of appeal' which chases up the idea with the function sitting on it.

The teams operate very successfully and have a bulletin, 'Leading Edge News', which keeps all the teams up to date on each team's new ideas. Although there are areas for improvement in the working of the teams, most, if not all, managers in this company would give the thumbs-up to their Leading Edge Teams.

In fact, the success of those teams involved directly with the external customers, was one factor which encouraged other functions to set up their own leading edge initiative. For example, finance set up its own teams.

The wider benefit of this initiative has been a clear statement about the importance of implementing ideas which directly or indirectly help and attract the customer – across the company. There is a clear demonstration of the company's values in action. And as all levels have participated there is a real sense of involvement and commitment to Leading Edge.

In this organisation the values of top management were

fairly well in line with what I hoped to achieve. With some other companies we have gone through a values audit and then decided what the values needed to be to ensure continuing and growing success. Only then have we gone ahead and introduced innovative mechanisms.

A Way Ahead

Two final points of practical interest. First there is the potential élitism of innovation teams. That is, although teams are always encouraged to invite ideas from those around them, non-team members may not be as forthcoming as one might have hoped. Rotation of team members may be one way round this.

'Brian', the innovation software, has provided some interesting insights into how computer-aided creativity software may be used at work. We are currently designing a new piece of innovation software, which will have the ability to help a problem-solver 'frame' opportunities – that is, bring the invisible 'white light' into vision, and 'reframe' problems. Such software may become an important aid to future innovation teams or individuals working on critical and difficult innovation issues. Such software can act like an innovation process consultant – that is, the person who takes a team through a structured process of creative problem-solving. Unstructured creativity sessions are usually chaotic and are one factor which has contributed to the poor image of 'creativity' training.

In conclusion, there are undoubtedly a plethora of mechanisms which can be used to stimulate creativity. I have touched on one or two types of Total Innovation interventions. Equally importantly, I have tried to indicate some of the background features of an organisation which will stifle or help nurture such innovation initiatives.

References

1. For a full introduction to 'mind maps' see:
   Buzan, T. *Use Your Head*, Ariel Books, 1982.
   Russell, P. *The Brain Book*, Hawthorn Books, 1979.
   Brown, M. *Memory Matters*, David & Charles, 1977.
2. Adams, J. L. *Conceptual Blockbusting*, 2nd edition, W. W. Norton & Company, 1979, p. 54.
3. See: Dreistadt, R. 'An analysis of the use of analogy and metaphor in science.' *Journal of Psychology*, 1968, 68, pp. 97–116.
   Necka, E. 'The use of analogy in creative problem solving.' *Polish Psychological Bulletin*, 1985, Vol. 16(4), pp. 245–255.
4. See: Lewin, K. *Resolving Social Conflicts: Selected Papers on Group Dynamics*. (Ed. Lewin, G. W.) Harper & Row, 1948.
   Lewin, K. 'Field Theory and Learning.' in *Field Theory in Social Science: Selected Theoretical Papers by Kurt Lewin*, Cartwright, D. (Ed.), Tavistock Publications, 1952.
5. An excellent insight into the way that our past experience may 'channel' our way of looking at the present is:
   Abercrombie, M. L. J. *The Anatomy of Judgement*, Penguin, 1969.
   Also see: de Bono, E. *The Mechanism of Mind*, Penguin, 1969.
6. For a review of creative problem solving techniques, see:
   Van Gundy, A. B. *Techniques of Structured Problem Solving*, Van Nostrand
   Reinhold, 2nd edition, 1988.
7. Many thanks to Ian Taylor for yet another fertile analogy.
8. See: Rickards, T. *Stimulating Innovation*, Frances Pinter, 1985, p. 54.
9. See: Prince, G.M. *The Practice of Creativity*, Harper & Row, New York, 1970.
10. See: Mansfield, R. S. & Busse, T. V. *The Psychology of Creativity and Discovery*, Nelson-Hall, 1981, pp. 123–124.
11. This technique comes from: Prince, G. M. Ibid.
12. Some, if not many practitioners of creative problem solving, may, at first sight, disagree with this apparent constraint. Continuing experience with Leading Edge Teams suggests that there is a tendency with some, if not many people, to lose focus at the 'blue' stage if criteria are not already established. My feeling is that the more a group really understands the problem, the less is the need to think through the criteria before going 'blue'. In this sense, identifying the criteria is, of itself, part of the problem definition.
13. Humourist and writer, Stephen Pile, invented the term.

14. Kolb, D. A. *Experiential Learning*, Prentice-Hall, 1984.
Kolb, D. A., Rubin, I. M., & McIntyre, J. M. (Eds.) *Organizational Psychology, readings on human behavior in organizations*, Prentice-Hall, fourth edition, 1984.
Kolb, D. A., Rubin, I. M., & McIntyre, J. M. (Eds.) *Organizational Psychology, an experiential approach to organizational behavior*, Prentice-Hall, fourth edition, 1984.
15. Belbin, M. *Management Teams*, Heinemann, 1981.

CHAPTER TEN

The Empowered Individual and Organisation

Certain attitudes can break a company. 'Rigid fingers' is one such attitude. As already mentioned, this describes the individual who explains why he cannot change things because of 'them' up there. He believes that what really creates change is 'them'. He sees himself as fairly – if not totally – powerless. What this individual forgets is that whilst one finger is pointing up, there are always three pointing firmly back at him.

Yet, time and again having fired people up with innovative enthusiasm, within an organisation, up pops the energy-sapping and much-shared 'yes . . . but' of 'My boss won't want it that way; the system; the company won't, the organisation won't; the partnership won't, the bank won't'.

Monolithic Giants Striding around the Mid-Atlantic

People start to talk about 'the company', 'the organisation' or simply state the name of their organisation 'IBM', or whoever, in a way which encourages you to believe that organisations *actually exist*. Now a sociologist may argue that a collection of individuals does begin to acquire characteristics not found in any one individual. This may be true. All the same, when

Figure 10.1   Rigid Fingers Galore!

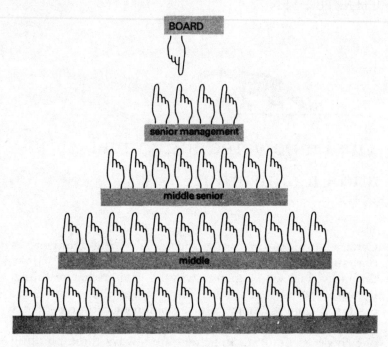

it comes to changing things, it takes *individuals* to start the ball rolling. Yet people refer to their organisations in such a disempowering way. They seem to regard the organisation as a monster with powers in its own right – independent of people. In one sense, an organisation is just a collection of individuals providing some service or product. *We are the organisation.*

I recall well working within a very traditional engineering-based group of companies. At various levels of management we attempted to stimulate innovation. The sessions went well at each level – at least until the end of each session – when 'rigid fingers' began to appear in abundance. Junior management saw middle management as symbolising 'yes . . . but' in action. Middle management vigorously denied that they were resistant to change. They identified middle-senior managers as the real dinosaurs. Middle senior management, in their turn, blamed senior management, describing them as political animals and powerful barons, who were too interested in maintaining their own power-base and therefore over-keen on protecting the status quo. As you have already guessed, senior management, in their turn, agreed that they would love to change things – but that the dinosaurs incarnate, not even dynamic dinosaurs, existed at the top.

So what did the top have to say for themselves? In reporting back to the Board on how people felt about the innovation initiatives, I explained that everyone tended to point the finger of blame at those immediately senior to themselves, and so ultimately they were pointing at the Board. At this point the managing director set about (politely) accusing two of his co-directors of being dinosaurs. They, in turn, accused their other colleagues. What had started as a very 'British' board meeting, had become a more truthful and vitriolic bloodletting.

The managing director made a key statement along the following lines:

> My deepest regret is that I hardly know of one man-
> ager who does not underestimate his zone of control
> and, more importantly, I certainly don't know of a
> single person who doesn't underestimate his zone of
> influence. [See Figure 10.2.] Therefore, when I feel
> we need to create change in the organisation, I feel
> that so often we are having to initiate it from the top.

At this point, the self-fulfilling nature of the myth becomes clear. Managers stand paralysed by this myth that they are not the organisation. Clearly an organisation is nothing more than a collection of potentially dynamic individuals along with some technology and service – and yet this energy is so easily lost, as people really begin to believe that the organisation exists as an independent being. And because there is a lack of creative 'friction' or energy within the organisation – senior managers are forced to initiate changes – thus proving the mind-set that it is 'they' up there, who always create change.

It would be instructive, if not depressing, at many companies' top management briefings, when the top 1,000 or so managers are present, to ask the following question:

Figure 10.2   Zones of Control and Influence

DISEMPOWERED
   PEOPLE

EMPOWERED PEOPLE

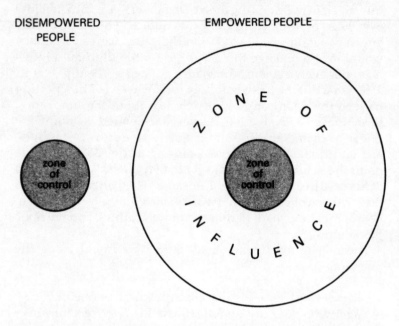

'Ladies and gentlemen, will those people who believe they
have little or no control or influence over what happens in
this organisation please stand up.' Although in many organisations the question would be quite unacceptable, providing
the first 50 or so stood up (and by doing so they would at least
show they were not completely disempowered), I guess, in
some organisations, 100, 200, 300, 500 and maybe practically
all of those top 1,000 managers would stand up. Thus they
would see the myth revealed. In this sense, if we believe that
the organisation happens to us, 'it' takes on a life of its own
and does therefore happen to us.

Psychostructure[1]

How can the 'organisation', in the sense of the values and
structure, disempower people? Perhaps, older-world, stuck
organisations look for people who are happy just to 'get on

and do their jobs' and so work primarily if not totally just within their area of control. Perhaps they recruit or mould folk who are not going to rock the boat – that is, people who won't act within their zone of influence.

The cause of disempowerment probably involves an interaction of people and the 'system' within which they work – that is the rules, norms and values that people, *en masse*, share.

Let us first of all consider the psychology of empowerment. Some people are very 'internal',[2] in that they consider what happens to them is, to a fairly high degree, down to them. Believing that their actions are effective in determining what happens in their life, they act accordingly. Thus we see a very deep self-fulfilling prophecy in action.

At the other end of the scale, there are those who see themselves as comparatively powerless or as the pawns[3] in life. Such 'externals' see control as being outside them. Either they believe that control lies with *others* – powerful and perhaps almost Kafkaesque others, or they believe it lies in the hands of *fate/chance/luck*. 'It's not what you know, it's who you know' captures the sense that it is powerful 'others' who really know what is going on and it is they who make and enable things to happen.

'It's a question of being in the right place at the right time; I wasn't born with a silver spoon in my mouth; just my luck; the gods will decide' – these expressions show the finger of blame pointing at 'fate', 'chance' and 'luck'!

Clearly those of us who see ourselves as powerless pawns in life's game will not try new and exciting moves on its chessboard. Rather like an autumn leaf, externals see themselves and their lives as determined by powerful and random forces that throw them high and then lash them violently to the ground. In which case, what's the point in trying to change things?

The individual's propensity to being internal – that is, empowered – or external – that is, disempowered, helpless and pawn-like, seems to be largely determined by experience in life, especially early on in life. Where the young child experiences that it can exert will and effort which results in desired outcomes, it starts to develop an internal view of events. It sees that outcomes are, in good part, determined by what he or she does. On the other hand, externals experience an early childhood where there is less opportunity to exercise free will or where the exercise of such will does not result in the desired outcome – or both. So, sure enough, if you can't influence things, why bother trying?

Consistent experience of having no control understandably creates a sense of helplessness and hopelessness. A belief that you have some control or choice over what happens is essential for psychological and physical well-being. Concerning longevity, for example, one study followed 55 women all over 65, where 17 had no alternative but to enter an old people's home. Of that 17, 8 died within four weeks of entry and 16 died within ten weeks. Only 1 of the other 38 who had alternatives to the home died in the same ten-week period.[4]

Internals seem more likely to be drawn to or create organisations which suit their belief that things can be changed for the better. A study of 33 business firms in the Montreal region found that the greater the internality score of the top executive, the more innovative that firm was. Such firms also changed their product lines more frequently and introduced a greater number of new products:

> Finally, whereas firms dominated by external managers made only incremental product modifications, firms with internal top executives were more prone to make dramatic changes in their product lines. The action orientation of internals in a managerial situation seems to have broad repercussions on the strategy of the firm.[5]

External managers and companies seem, perhaps, ill equipped to deal with a world of fast change. Externals suit well an unchanging, more conservative environment. Internals are more at ease in managing change and its associated turmoil.

Therefore the question is raised as to what, if anything, can be done to increase internality or this sense of empowerment. For example, it appears that comparatively short and practical training programmes in 'generic problem-solving techniques' can increase people's sense of internality and emotional stability – and actually give rise to objective improvement in performance, in this case the obtaining of higher-standard university degrees.[6]

I recall one experiment where I gave £50 to a team of three managers with the challenge that, without doing anything illegal and without simply borrowing money, they turn the £50 into £1,000 within twenty-four hours! (I had gleaned the idea of the challenge from a similar experiment in another company.[7]) The look on the three managers' faces was a delight to behold. The challenge looked next to impossible. If they could achieve this target, what might such success say for bringing about seemingly impossible changes within their organisation. Twenty-four hours later they had made in excess of £1,000. However, this kind of exercise may not, unless then applied to real problems, transfer back to work. That is, awareness and understanding do not of themselves ensure transfer.

But what about the structure and style of the organisation itself – how can this be designed to empower people? Not surprisingly, the more we treat people as people and not pawns or cogs the better they perform. Although changes within the organisation will not necessarily help empower those people who feel personally very disempowered, there are many people who will take the opportunity of greater control, if offered. As Richard E. Walton, Professor of Business Administration at Harvard Business School, stresses,[8] fixed job definitions, excessive top–down controls, a hierarchy riddled with status symbols, where employees are seen as a cost and informed on a 'need to know' basis, all seem to be a sure way to create disempowerment and alienation. Whereas flexible definitions of jobs, with flatter organisational structures, where status is minimised, where people are valued as the primary and ever developable asset and not simply as a cost – and informed and involved widely – these are the conditions which create a greater sense of empowerment and commitment.

Tickling or Transforming the Dinosaur

Many of these changes require a central shift in values. Within an organisation there is usually a minority of individuals who are challenging the existing values. Some of these people would probably want to knock any system – that is, there are always going to be a handful of dedicated malcontents, but the others may be indicating the direction in which you need to move. These individuals are, however, running against the tide of the culture and may, if successful, become harbingers of change, or, if unsuccessful, become organisational lepers.

So, if you see yourself as a rebel and want to bring about change, what do you need to do to ensure that the dinosaur doesn't just sit on top of you? Successful rebels are excellent 'guerrilla fighters'. They understand when and how to move. They have a strong sense of the worlds inhabited by those who need to be influenced. They adapt to those different worlds. But, all the same, if they are too innovative and empowered for the organisation they wish to influence, their impatience may be their downfall.

Figure 10.3   Empowerment/Values Grid

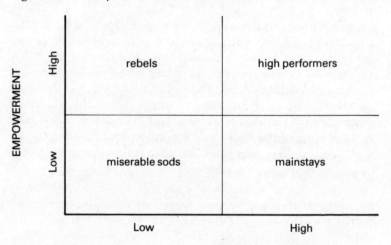

But the odd question is this. Why should there be just a few or a minority of people trying to tickle the dinosaur? Usually there are many people who recognise that there is a need for change – but these people are pointing their fingers at others. Are you pointing your finger? And in the meantime who is pointing the finger of blame at you? Who is complaining that, much as they would love to change things, there is a real block, a total 'yes . . . butting' dinosaur – you. In most organisations, people are fast to see themselves as Type 2 thinkers, condemning most others to the ranks of disempowered Type 1 dinosaurs. How come most of us think that it is everyone else who is stuck?

The Fun Audit

In a world of change, organisations which will survive and thrive are those which are fast to adapt. Very successful organisations are beginning to initiate the changes and not simply respond to them. An organisation which has low energy, poor values and motivational matches, where 'punters' encounter that all-pervading sense of 'I just work here' – is slow to adapt to change, if it ever does adapt at all. Why – because people don't care; their hearts are not in it – and why should they be? Successful organisations need to attend to two key features of their success – fun and profit (or, in the case of non-commercial organisations – meeting their non-financial objectives).

When we are aligned with our work and our places of work, when we are involved and sensitive to our customers, when we remain unstuck in our thinking and so constantly find new and better ways of providing appropriate services and products – then we are unstoppable. We achieve our organisational aims and enjoy ourselves. Productive fun is the name of the game. And whereas most organisations are appropriately concerned about financial tracking and auditing – the concrete output of the system – too few audit and monitor the real heart of the organisation – people. They need a 'productive fun' audit to run alongside the financial one. Only then can they ensure that they stay on track.

This book has touched on a range of ideas and practices you and your colleagues can try out. The list is far from exhaustive – and some of the ideas themselves may be proven wrong with time or may become outdated. However, there is a single underlying theme throughout the book – keep thinking and don't get stuck with the way you think. The Type 2 manager has the ability to generate new solutions and spot new opportunities. There is no simple formula, but there is an underlying awareness which can create the solutions you need for today – and then a new one for tomorrow.

It would be completely inappropriate to wish you well with trying out some of the ideas in this book – and with your own future generally – as this would suggest a very external or pawn-like existence. As one famous golfer said, when asked whether or not he believed in luck, 'I practise at being lucky and the more I practise the luckier I become.'[9]

References

1. 'Psychostructure' describes the process whereby managers are selected and moulded so as to fit the structure of the firm. See: Maccoby, M. *The Gamesman*, Bantam, 1977.
2. For a sound introduction to the idea of 'locus of control', see: Lefourt, H. M. *Locus of Control*, Lawrence Erlbaum Associates, 1982.
3. Very similar to the idea of 'locus of control' is that of 'origins and pawns'. See: de Charms, R. *Personal Causation*, Academic Press, 1968.
4. Bakal, D. A. *Psychology and Medicine*, Tavistock Publications, 1979, p.103.
5. Miller, D., Kets de Vries, M. F. R. & Toulouse, J. 'Top executive locus of control and its relationship to strategy-making, structure and environment.' *Academy of Management Journal*, 1982, Vol. 25, No. 2, pp. 237–253.
6. Duckworth, D. H. 'Evaluation of a programme for increasing the effectiveness of personal problem-solving.' *British Journal of Psychology*, 1983, 74, pp. 119–127.
   This programme could well be adapted for people at work, so as to increase their sense of internality and empowerment.

7. Many thanks to Ivan Williams, Marlow Association, for this idea.
   See his paper:
   'Creativity Groups', as presented at the Economist Conference,
   'Intrapreneurship in Practice', April 20th–22nd, 1986.
8. Walton, R. E. 'From control to commitment in the workplace.'
   Harvard Business Review, March–April, 1985, pp. 77–84.
   See the excellent section on the transitional stage from an old to a
   new world organisation.
9. I believe Gary Player said this.

If you would like to receive information on our consultancy services, seminars, publications and learning packages (based upon the ideas and practices described in this book) simply write to:

Customer Information Manager
Innovation Centre Europe Ltd
BCM Box 6
London WC1N 3XX
England
Tel: 0491 411173

INDEX

IDEA 1

today	week 1		
month 1	month 3	month 6	month 9

week 2		week 3		

year 1	year 2	year 3	year 4	year 5

DECISION:

IDEA 1

today		week 1	
month 1	month 3	month 6	month 9

week 2		week 3		

year 1	year 2	year 3	year 4	year 5

DECISION:

IDEA 1

today	week 1

month 1	month 3	month 6	month 9

week 2	week 3

year 1	year 2	year 3	year 4	year 5

DECISION:

IDEA 1

today		week 1	
month 1	**month 3**	**month 6**	**month 9**

week 2	week 3

year 1	year 2	year 3	year 4	year 5

DECISION: